A WORKSHOP OF THE POSSIBLE

A WORKSHOP OF THE POSSIBLE

Nurturing Children's Creative Development

Ruth Shagoury Hubbard

STENHOUSE PUBLISHERS

YORK, MAINE

Stenhouse Publishers, 226 York Street, York, Maine 03909

Credits:

Page 16–17: from "Building Generative Curriculum," by Lester L. Laminack and Sandra Lawing, *Primary Voices K–6*, August 1994. Copyright 1994 by the National Council of Teachers of English. Reprinted with permission.
Page 19: from *Inventing a Classroom*, by Kathryn Whitmore and Caryl Crowell, Stenhouse Publishers, York, ME. Copyright 1994 Kathryn Whitmore and Caryl Crowell. Reprinted with permission.

Library of Congress Cataloging-in-Publication Data

Hubbard, Ruth, 1950-
    A workshop of the possible : nurturing children's creative
  development / Ruth Shagoury Hubbard.
      p. cm.
    Includes bibliographical references and index.
    ISBN 1-57110-007-5 (alk. paper)
    1. Creative thinking.   2. Creative ability in children.   3. Open
  plan schools—United States—Case studies.   I. Title.
  LB1062.H75   1996
  370.15'7—dc20   95-40916
                                         CIP

Cover and interior design by Ron Kosciak, *Dragonfly Design*
Cover and insert photographs by Jim Whitney
Typeset by Octal Publishing, Inc.

Manufactured in the United States of America on acid-free paper
99 98 97 96 8 7 6 5 4 3 2 1

To Meghan, Nathan, and Cory

with thanks for all you have taught me
and with more love than you can imagine

Contents

Acknowledgments

My first thanks go to the children whose stories are told in these pages. They have been unfailingly patient with me, willing to take the time to explain their thinking and ideas. I am honored by their trust, their patience, and their good humor.

I would not have had the opportunity to learn from these children if it weren't for teachers like Pat McLure, Nancy Winterbourne, Leslie Funkhouser, and Jill Ostrow, who graciously opened their classroom doors to me. In the midst of their busy professional lives, these extraordinary teachers shared their reflections on children and learning, talking with me before and after school, and often in phone conversations long into the night. I am grateful for their wisdom and for the friendships we've forged.

My writing community nourishes me and keeps me going; they tell me what works, and—thank God!—what doesn't. I would like to thank Brenda Power, Jill Ostrow, Mary Burke-Hengen, Andra Makler, Nancy Winterbourne, Carol Lauritzen, Linda Christensen, Nancy Nagel, Caryl Hurtig, and Tom Romano for reading drafts of this book and helping me with their thoughtful comments. Their suggestions and enthusiasm always made me eager to dive back into the writing.

Special thanks to the members of the Fairbanks branch of the Alaska Teacher Research Network, who helped me in my final revisions. Terri Austin's home served as our retreat center, and gave me the luxury of talking through my ideas with a group of innovative teachers. We wrote and talked, ate and laughed under June's midnight sun. Suggestions from Terri Austin, Bonnie Gaborik, Cindee Karns, Annie Keep-Barnes, Janelle McCrackin, Barb Smith, and Karen Stapf-Harris are woven throughout the fabric of the book.

The most important support has come from my family. They have encouraged me in every phase, ever willing to put aside their own work to talk through ideas with me, suggest books or articles, cook scones for me, or share great tunes. Though he was busy applying to college and finishing his senior year, Nathan was especially generous with his time, reading every draft, helping me play with words and sentences, and inspiring me with his own creativity and wit.

Jim Whitney provided the extra support that comes from his always generous spirit. His photographs show his careful eye and his respect for children. One of the hardest tasks was to choose from the incredible images he captured from Jill's room. Besides taking pictures, he immersed himself in every phase of the project, even nudging me to learn to use new software, which I will now admit was worth the struggle.

No one could have a better editor than Philippa Stratton. Her faith in the project kept me on track when I got discouraged. She took the time to talk through my half-formed ideas with me, suggest books, articles, and movies that would inform my work, and best of all, she read everything I wrote—even my earliest drafts—and helped me shape a new whole I had not imagined at the start.

Brenda Miller Power not only acted as reader and editor, she also was my cheerleader and critic, as only a best friend can be. Across three thousand miles, we managed to communicate by fax, phone, and E-mail several times a week. Thanks, Brenda! If there is such a thing as a muse, you're it!

Jill Ostrow is the most influential teacher I have ever had. I continue to learn from her every day as she stretches my knowledge of what children can do. My three years in her classroom frame the ways I think about what is possible in public schools. Jill is a unique combination of passionate child advocate, insightful teacher, hilarious comedian, and revolutionary theorist. I am grateful for her teaching and writing contributions and, most of all, for her warm friendship.

1

Respecting Children's Creativity

What makes the difference between an outstandingly creative person and a less creative one is not any special power but greater knowledge (in the form of practiced expertise) and the motivation to acquire and use it.

MARGARET BODEN

When my daughter Meg was a young child not yet in school, I remember hurrying her out the door one crisp fall morning, my hands full of books and supplies for my classroom and thoughts on the morning ahead of me. Rather than going directly to the car as I wanted her to do, Meg dropped her backpack on the steps, kneeled on the cold frost-covered ground and exclaimed, "Oh, Mummy, the grass is all different! Today, it's tiny silver swords!" As I knelt beside her to exclaim over the transformation, I marveled at her metaphor and delighted in the way her creativity had helped me see the world in a new way that busy morning.

What does it mean to be creative? The image that comes to mind for many of us is the "creative genius" who takes up paintbrush, pen, or violin and, inspired by the muse, looks at the world in a completely new way and creates outstanding art—art that is much better than anything we normal folks could do. But creativity is part of everyone's natural abilities. When a child sees the grass as tiny silver swords, she is making a novel association, a thought that didn't exist in her mind before. We have only to notice the problem-solving and original insights that are part of young children's daily lives to realize that creativity plays a key role in human existence.

We can learn so much from children. As a teacher, I watch young people as they embark on their mental adventures, generating ideas and possibilities. They surprise and fascinate me with their abilities and their different ways of making sense of the world. Early in my teaching career, I often underestimated children's true capabilities. Margaret Boden, a British psychologist, remarks that this is not unusual:

> A young child's ability to construct new conceptual spaces is seldom appreciated, even by its doting parents. All human infants spontaneously transform their own conceptual space in fundamental ways, so that they come to be able to think thoughts of a kind which they could not have thought before. Their creative powers gradually increase, as they develop the ability to vary their behavior in more and more flexible ways, and even to reflect on what they are doing. (Boden 1991, p. 63)

CREATIVITY AND THE YOUNG CHILD

It isn't surprising that parents and caregivers would underestimate a young child's abilities. Psychologists have only recently begun to appreciate the extent of young children's creative capabilities. Thirty years ago, the dominant view in child psychology was that children under seven years of age were in many ways extremely limited in their abilities to think and reason. The work of Jean Piaget and his colleagues was the most influential in the field. In *Children's Minds,* her pioneer book on children's thinking, Margaret Donaldson sums up the prevailing attitude: "By the mid-1960's, a flood of researches had been pouring out of Geneva for years, all of them tending to the same conclusion: the child under seven is very restricted intellectually. He has developed considerable skills on a practical level, mastering these rapidly during the first eighteen months of his life. But he is not much of a thinker" (Donaldson 1978, p. 28).

The first challenge to these theories came about as language theorists began to take a closer look at the ways children learn and use language. Noam Chomsky's (1965) claim that children could actually work out and use the very complex systems of human languages was in direct opposition to the prevailing beliefs about children's abilities. Indeed, Chomsky himself proposed that children must have a "highly specific" ability, related only to language, which he ultimately named the Language Acquisition Device (LAD).

But ideas about children's creative capabilities are changing rapidly. Many current theorists believe that the extraordinary thinking and reasoning skills children use to learn language are not limited to language learning alone (Donaldson 1978; Stern 1990). According to child psychologist Daniel Stern, children as young as two can associate one experience with another—not only across space, but also across time. And, Stern asserts, this can occur even before they have developed language. "It now seems that non-verbal, even global, experiences can also be remembered and represented without being transposed into words. And associations between these nonverbal representations can be made to form complex networks" (Stern 1990, p. 124). Researcher John Macnamara (1972) believes that children can learn language precisely because they possess other skills.

Even very young children exhibit far more advanced abilities than we had believed in the past. In the current revolution in infant psychology, scientists are finally beginning to learn to "ask babies questions they could actually answer" (Stern 1990, p. 5). Daniel Stern's research shows that infants and young children are far from the passive beings we once thought. They are able to regulate face-to-face interactions as early as four months of age and use this ability to "train" their caregivers to give them the amount of stimulation that their personalities require (Stern 1985).

Creativity involves these abilities to explore, evaluate, and make associations. In fact, much recent research supports the view that creativity is not one specific power, but an aspect of intelligence in general (Papert 1980; Perkins 1981; Gardner 1983; Schank and Childers 1988). In this view, creativity is defined as part of our natural thinking strategies, including such abilities as problem solving, novel associations, and insights.

As human beings, then, we all share degrees of creative power as part of our everyday lives. Unfortunately, this is not the view that has been traditionally emphasized in schools. Instead of building on the natural creativity of young children and providing them with the practice and motivation they need to stretch their abilities, schools typically train young children to be passive students. In his disturbing preschool ethnography "Learning the Student Role: Kindergarten as Academic Boot Camp," Harry Gracey (1967) concludes that "while children's perceptions of the world and opportunities for genuine spontaneity and creativity are being systematically eliminated from the kindergarten, unquestioned obedience to authority and rote learning of meaningless material are being encouraged" (p. 253).

Fortunately, recent trends in instruction are beginning to take seriously the notion that children need to use their minds flexibly, make creative leaps in their thinking, and take the initiative in their learning. Rather than relying on rote learning and canned curricula, a child-centered, response-based, holistic philosophy of instruction opens the door to students' using and developing their own voices in new, creative ways.

My belief in the importance of understanding children's creative capabilities has grown stronger over the years. When I went back to school to become a teacher of teachers, I knew that an important part of my mission was to come to understand children's creative development and the classroom settings that work to nurture it. As part of my graduate work at the University of New Hampshire, I was fortunate to be able to spend extended time in classrooms so that I could talk with children in the midst of their learning, in their daily environments rather than in an experimental setting. First-grade teacher Patricia McLure became my mentor as she allowed me to become a member of her classroom community three mornings a week for over two years, learning with and from the children. They taught me about their world from their points of view (Hubbard 1989). And I learned from Pat—how and why she set up the classroom environment to meet her children's needs and capabilities, how she adapted her instruction based on what she learned from them, and what her role as teacher was in nurturing her students' creative development.

The lessons I learned from Pat and her students set me on a path to continue to learn in public school classrooms in extended studies from the inside out, with teachers who consciously reflect on their children's learning strategies as well as their own. Besides laying a foundation for my ways of working within classrooms, my research in Pat's room also made it clear to me that if I want to understand what children are truly capable of doing, I need to be in settings where the teacher's philosophy allows kids to initiate a great deal of their own learning.

Since that time, I have been privileged to work in several classrooms for prolonged studies. Besides Pat McLure's first-grade classroom, I spent two years in Leslie Funkhouser's second grade and two years in Nancy Winterbourne's second grade, and I am currently completing my third year in Jill Ostrow's multi-age primary classroom. In these pages you will hear voices and stories from these school communities. (Although I have used the names of the teachers, with their permission, I have changed the names of all the classroom children in keeping with the preference of some of their parents.) The teachers' and children's personalities, as well as the classroom settings, are very different from each other, yet I was able to discover certain patterns that have enabled me to begin to formulate elements that work together to create rich learning environments.

In this book, I share examples of what is possible for children when they work with teachers in environments that nurture and respect their creative abilities. My aim is to introduce readers to real classrooms and real children, so that through these stories we can tease out the elements that together create a "workshop of the possible." I hope these stories will help educators look at children with renewed respect, and work with them to transform classrooms.

MY ROLE AS RESEARCHER

 In my role as researcher, I view the classrooms in which I work as their own culture, and the children teach me as "ethnographic informants." Ethnography is the work of describing a culture, with the goal "to grasp the native's point of view, his relation to life, to realize *his* vision of *his* world" (Malinowski 1922, p. 25). The way the ethnographer learns a culture is through his or her informant, a native speaker who acts as a source of information. The informant literally becomes the ethnographer's teacher. If we invite children to become our ethnographic informants, we can begin to understand their world on their own terms, without falling prey to preexisting assumptions about their abilities. In this role, the child is not the passive subject of the research, but an active collaborator.

In the classrooms in which I have worked, I have been a participant as well as an observer from the first day of school in September. I take part in the workshops and projects the children are working on, and I also circulate around the room, talking with the children about what they are doing and interviewing them about their processes. I audiotape conversations that children have among themselves and with me, as well as many whole-group class discussions. I also sketch classroom setups and children at work, and I document where and with whom the children choose to work.

While I interview and interact with all the children in the classroom, I usually choose three to five main informants each year with whom I spend the most time. How do I choose these children? It evolves naturally: children who are comfortable talking with me often, children who intrigue me, children who show a range of different strategies, and often children that the teacher is concerned about and would like me to spend more time with.

My role in the classroom evolves over time as well, and it is never exactly the same. In Pat McLure's room, I was more like a bigger kid in the class. Because I was there most days of the week and was clearly in the role of a learner, the children did not perceive me at all as an authority figure; in fact, one of them asked me how I liked being a "teacher's maid," and another asked me how many more years I would need to be in first grade!

Jill Ostrow's classroom is currently the classroom I know best. For the last three years I have been a member of this class at least one full day per week. My involvement with the class has covered a wide range: reading and writing stories and investigating math patterns, interviewing children about

their work and ideas, joining in on the tire swinging at recess, building
bridges out of string, toilet paper and popsicle sticks, going on field trips,
and attending potluck family gatherings. Because the children stay with Jill
from first through third grade, I have come to know the children, and many
of the families, quite well. They expect me to ask questions, take notes, and
join in the classroom activities, including recess duty and occasionally covering for Jill.

Jenna, one of my main informants, described my role in the class as a kind
of "teaching assistant" in one story she wrote, recorded in her invented
spelling below:

> Hello, my name is Jenna (pernounced Jen-u) and I am going to tell you about
> Ruth. Ruth is the "assistant teacher" as I call her. Ruth is studying how kids
> learn but I can't understand why because she was a kid once and she had to
> learn too. And now she is old and greay and very wise. (I diddent mean the
> old and greay part, Ruth) When I said that she started laughing and said,
> "That is OK it did not hurt my feelings." Anyway, let's get back to the story.

The children became used to my constant note taking, often kidding me
about my "messy cursive that's hard to read" or telling me, "You should be
taking notes now, 'cause this is interesting," or encouraging me to improve
my rough sketches (see Figure 1.1). Early this year, I was sitting in as Maria,
whom I have known for three years, was writing with a new first-grade student, Ailene. "How come you're writing?" Ailene asked me.

"'Cause I'm trying to learn how you think and work," I told her. "What's
going on in your head."

Ailene looked puzzled. "You can't know what goes on in our heads."

"Well, I can try to learn."

Maria leapt into the discussion at that point. "She *does* know what's in my
head, 'cause she's been here from when I was in first grade, then second
grade, then now."

"What helps me figure it out, Maria?"

"I think sitting. Listening. Writing. Seeing the problems we do. And
sketching. That's pretty hard, and you don't put in the eyes yet, but you can
get better. I'm getting better. Now, I'm gonna draw this girl who worked
long long long hours in the fields and prob'ly didn't get to take too many
baths." With that, she was back, immersed in her own story.

I hope you will come to know Maria and the other children as I describe
what I've learned from sitting, listening, writing, and sketching with them
over the years. While my data come from all the classrooms I have worked
in, the most extended examples in each chapter are from Jill Ostrow's multi-
age community of learners. A good companion to this book is *A Room with a
Different View*, Jill's story of one year in her classroom and the formation of a

Figure 1.1   A sample page from Ruth's fieldnotes

multi-age community. Her book explains more of the details of her philosophy of teaching, as well as her project plans, her assessment strategies, and
the ways she works with children, parents, and other members of the educational community.

   In *A Workshop of the Possible*, I delineate the categories that have emerged
from my fieldwork in classrooms over the last decade. In Chapters 2 through 5
I discuss key elements that are vital in the workshop environment. Chapters 6

through 8 move into the invisible workshops that are going on inside the children's minds. In the last chapter I explain how all these elements work in concert when the curriculum grows out of children's abilities to pose problems and uses inquiry to drive their development.

This book is only a beginning. I'm afraid Jenna was right when she noted, "There could be a creativity book written with 100,000 pages, and there still wouldn't be enough pages for all the children's ideas." Still, I invite you to enter these classrooms with me and learn from the stories and experiences of many teachers and students as we delight in, puzzle over, and attempt to understand children's extraordinary creative abilities.

2

Creating Classroom Environments: Special Rules and Extraordinary Events

Like a young turtle, Bobby tucks his head into his jersey, covering his chin with the material, then slowly extends his neck and stretches back his head. A hastily torn off sweater has mussed his hair, causing red tufts to stand out in all directions, but he is oblivious. His body moves slowly, absently; he is lost in thought, staring straight ahead instead of down at the writing folder before him.

The noise of a chair scraping on the floor breaks his trance, and his eyes meet mine.

"You look like you're thinking hard this morning."

Bobby nods and licks his chapped lips. "I'm trying to remember what it was like at the soccer game I was writing about."

"How do you do that?"

A pause. "Um . . . think about it. Try to remember . . . I sort of see it, but I can't remember if there was another guy on the team *there*." His finger jabs at an open space on the white soccer field. "I think he *should* be there." His voice trails off, and he rapidly sketches in the outline of a bulky player, upside down, lunging toward a ball.

"We almost got a goal," he writes slowly, sounding each word aloud.

Bobby is hard at work, reasoning, remembering, thinking, evaluating . . . *creating*. He doesn't know how lucky he is. He could be in a classroom like the one of my friend Carla, who remembers sitting in school similarly lost in thought, but being jarred to consciousness by a teacher's harsh voice: "Carla, what are you doing?"

"I'm thinking," she responded truthfully.

"Well, stop it," her teacher snapped.

Classrooms like Carla's are still too common; the thinking is that there's not enough time for the kind of serious work in which Bobby was engaged. An efficiency expert would no doubt rate Bobby's efforts as time off task, nothing of significance. Yet Bobby was incredibly conscientious in his writing efforts, trying to recreate realistically the scene he was writing about. He worked to organize his drawing and his words to represent the action that took place.

Fortunately, Bobby is in a class that values process as well as product. His teacher, Patricia McLure, has set up a structure where he has the time to work on his projects at his own pace, not in a lockstep order where all the students are expected to follow the same time line. In Pat's writing and reading workshops, the students have a predictable structure where they can depend on working at their own individual pace from day to day; this makes an enormous difference in their growth as independent learners (Hubbard 1986). In classes like these, students like Bobby have the time they need to reach into their minds, recalling memories or concentrating on the particular issues involved in their projects. They aren't seen as off task; rather, they are seen as making the necessary creative space for their thinking.

Nancy Winterbourne, another teacher whose classroom is based on holistic philosophies in all areas of her curriculum, has gone a step further in providing a space within her classroom for children to take the time for sustained, uninterrupted thought. In one corner of her room, a dream-catcher hangs. This Native American symbol is a small woven circle whose net "catches" good dreams and subconscious thoughts, then funnels them through a small hole in the center and down a feather into the dreamer's mind. Bad dreams and thoughts are caught in the net, too, but are not allowed through the hole. The children in Nancy's classroom know that when they want to be undisturbed to pursue their thoughts and daydreams, they can sit in the rocking chair under the dream-catcher and take the time they need (Winterbourne and Hubbard 1990).

Teachers like Pat McLure and Nancy Winterbourne recognize that structuring the time within the classroom to individuals' needs and values is a vital part of what Vera John-Steiner calls the "invisible tools of creativity" (John-Steiner 1985). In her study of the processes of creative thinkers, she found that they all required *time* for sustained productive work and the practice of their craft, time for immersion in their interests and obsessions. These thinkers described the various ways they learned to structure their time and space or, as John-Steiner calls it, build their "houses of thought." Similarly, children need an atmosphere where they can develop a disciplined approach to their creative work, with time to support their working habits.

ORGANIZING TIME FOR PREDICTABILITY AND FLEXIBILITY

Creativity is best nurtured in an environment that has a great deal of both structure and freedom. Is such an environment possible? *Flexible predictability* may sound paradoxical, yet it is this condition that I see as vital in creating the kind of time that allows sustained and productive creative work to flourish.

In Pat McLure's primary classroom, the children know that each morning will begin with writing. "We do writing first thing in the morning every day," Pat explains. "Having it every morning at the same time, they know what they're going to be doing; it's something they can count on. They talk about ideas for their stories with their parents and they're thinking about what to write when they're on the way to school in the morning. They usually come in with something on their minds they can come in and write about. So, it's worked very nicely for us to do it first thing in the morning" (from an interview with Pat McLure, *Time and Choice* 1986. Graves and Hansen, producers).

Pat stresses the benefits of a daily routine for her students' creative processes. Because they expect writing time each day, they begin planning and thinking about their writing ideas before they start the writing itself. I see the benefits of this structure for myself; I, too, begin my day with writing. I often wake up thinking about where I left off yesterday and how I will proceed today. Fleeting insights or tidbits that I might not remember otherwise become part of the record of my daily thinking and writing. As I read the newspaper in the morning, I find myself making connections to whatever theme is prominent in my current writing. My mind seizes on an anecdote or fact I read or notice, and it helps me see my data from different perspectives. My daily routine allows me to make the transition to a different state as I prepare to enter my work space.

The violinist and composer Stephen Nachmanovitch writes about the importance of his routine in being able to enter the *temenos:*

> I find, paradoxically, that in preparing to create I am already creating . . . The specific preparations begin when I enter the *temenos*, the play space. In ancient Greek thought, the *temenos* is a magic circle, a delineated sacred space within

which special rules apply and in which extraordinary events are free to occur. My studio, or whatever space I work in, is a laboratory in which I experiment with my own consciousness. (Nachmanovitch 1990, pp. 74–75)

Within the routine in Pat's room, "extraordinary events are free to occur" because there is also a great deal of flexibility. Each child is not at the same point in the composing process during writing time. Instead, every writer progresses as the writing itself demands. Six-year-old Nick worked on the same piece about his fish ("My Aquarium") for over two months. Every day he added new descriptions of the fish or the setup of the tank or anecdotes about the fish trying to jump out of the tank. At the same time, his classmate Sasha tended to write short pieces that she finished every two or three days. Many other children began new pieces each day, writing and drawing the important experiences of their lives in a more journal-like format. Children working side by side can work on their own projects at their own pace: one student might be beginning a new piece, while another might be concluding one by working on the "About the Author" section or decorating a cover. All have the flexibility for sustained, productive work.

They can also depend on response from Pat, knowing that each week she will meet with them individually in brief writing conferences on whatever writing they are composing. What is also predictable is the general format of the conference: they know she will ask them to read their work, talk about the ideas and the experiences that make up the content of their stories, question them about parts she doesn't understand, and bring closure to the conference by finding out what they plan to do as their next step.

Yet at the same time the conferences allow for extreme flexibility. There is no standard list of questions used for every conference; each question or comment depends on the individual child and the demands of the particular piece of writing he or she is engaged in composing. Even the duration of the conferences varies greatly: some might be as brief as one minute (if the child is immersed in the work and Pat mostly wants to check in to see how it is going); others might stretch to as long as seven or eight minutes (if a child wants to explain an incident in more depth or reread an extended piece in its entirety). Sometimes Pat sees a perfect opportunity to teach a certain writing convention that would help make the student's meaning clearer; this, too, might stretch the length of the individual conference. Pat is guided by her knowledge of the children: the history of this child as a writer and the history of the particular piece of writing he or she is working on.

Even relatively small segments of time that are part of a routine can make a big difference in children's abilities to stretch their thinking. For example, in Jill Ostrow's multi-age class, daily Calendar Time includes a predictable time to experiment with numbers. Each morning at 10:30, they come together to mark off days on the calendar and explore the numbers and patterns that exist. Creativity is about being able to push your mind further and further, not narrow yourself down to one answer and be done. These children push themselves for as many ways to create the day's date as possible. Children take turns leading the activity, but each child knows that he or she is expected to manipulate the day's date as well as explore a "fraction of the day."

One September 28, Daniel was orchestrating Calendar Time. After waiting for his audience to be quiet, he stood at the whiteboard, ready to write down the different ways to make the number "28." As children called out their contributions, he wrote them down:

SHAUNA: 29 take away 1

JEREMY: 31 take away 3

KELLY: 41 take away 21 take away 1 and add 9

FIONA: 27 plus 1

JENNA: 56 divided by 2

MARIA: 30 take away 2

HANNAH: 25 plus 3

JENNIFER: 10 plus 10 plus 8

TARA: (10 times 2), put the parentheses things, then add 8

In this daily manipulation of numbers, the children create equations that match their understanding of mathematical concepts. From ages five through nine, and at all ability levels, they are able to contribute. They are exposed to some number sentences that they don't yet understand, but they become familiar with the language and terminology. And as a class, they continue to construct meaning together. For example, when Jenna said "divided by," Daniel was unsure how to make a "divided-by sign." "It's a minus sign with a dot on the top and bottom," Jenna explained. Ben is just beginning to explore the concept of counting and numbers. His contributions are applauded—and expanded upon, as this excerpt from my fieldnotes shows:

DANIEL: Ben?

BEN: 28 plus 20 . . .

JILL: OK, then . . . ?

KELLY: Take away 20.

(Daniel writes "28 + 20 − 20" on the whiteboard.)

JILL: Good job, Ben and Kelly!

During Calendar Time, the children also know they will be expected to come up with "fractions of the day." Right now, they are creating "people fractions," based on the number of people in the room. They come into school looking at their classmates, counting, and coming up with a variety of different fractions:

MICAH: 1 out of 28 people have a Cub Scout uniform on.

ESPERANZA: 10 out of 28 have short sleeves.

TRAVIS: 2 out of 28 have hats on.

FIONA: 5 out of 28 have ponytails.

JON: 2 out of 28 are sitting in the grey chair.

As each child states his or her "people fraction," Daniel writes it on the whiteboard in fraction form.

These two daily predictable times are set aside for playing with numbers. They take less than ten minutes altogether, yet provide important mathematical thinking time for the children. Within this structure, they are not looking for one right answer; instead, they are looking for an infinity of possible ways to represent different numbers or fractions. Listening to these math shares and the informal conversations that surround them has given me insight into ways that the children process information and create even more mathematical concepts than their responses demonstrate. On this particular day, Maria had a people fraction in her mind: 3 out of 28 kids have glasses on. But she didn't get called on. She also had two ways to represent 28; she got to say one of them. Tegan confided to me, "I had to keep thinking of three new ones, 'cause somebody said mine." Rather than being discouraged that their contribution has been stated by another, these children instead challenged themselves to think of others.

Just as the children in Pat's class prepare for their writing because of a daily predictable routine, the children in Jill's class come to school thinking of numbers and mentally manipulating them. They are thinking mathematically. In a sense, the children in Jill's class have entered a *temenos* like the one Nachmanovitch describes: a "space within which special rules apply and in which extraordinary events are free to occur."

ORGANIZING THE PHYSICAL SPACE

 The physical space is an essential consideration in providing the kind of time that children need for their work. The key is *access:* access to a range of working spaces, access to materials, access to other kids and other adults; these in turn give students access to their own creative processes.

Access to Work Spaces

In order to nurture children's creative development, we need to develop environments that provide different working spaces to meet the demands of children's particular tasks and ways of making meaning. In workshop classrooms where children's engagement flourishes, teachers have structured their classrooms so that these different spaces are a prominent feature. Rather than having assigned seats or desks, children are considered to be members of a wider creative workshop community, and sit where and with whom they need to.

Teachers create the landscapes of their classrooms with many conditions in mind. The look and feel of classrooms that contain areas such as the ones described here reflect the teachers' beliefs in these conditions for learning. Children have the flexibility to change where they are working depending on the needs and nature of their tasks. They can work alone when they need undisturbed time, or they can seek out spaces that accommodate two or three others to help or to share ideas. This in turn leads to far greater independence within the class; children know they can turn to others besides the teacher for help and feedback and are likely to work toward solving their problems as part of a community, rather than passively sit at their desks and wait for the teacher's help.

Walking into a classroom with this kind of flow and movement can be disconcerting to parents—and some teachers—the first time they experience it. But as I watch and document the involvement in work that goes on, it is clear that these conditions add to students' abilities to work for longer periods of time than many adults imagine.

I know this from firsthand experience, too. I think of my own writing process as I worked on this book. Sometimes I needed to spread out materials on the floor or on a large table. At other times, I wanted to retreat to a cozy corner and read and reread materials that stimulate my thinking and imagination. I alternated between writing stream-of-consciousness ideas in a journal and sitting down at the computer to compose. When I needed response or a chance to talk through my ideas, I picked up the phone to have an impromptu conference with a writing friend. I also met with a group of writers who share our work and give each other feedback. In short, I need *spaces* to work, not one designated space. I find I need the chance to get up and stretch out when I have been sitting in one place for too long. Or I might need to sit and stare into space undisturbed.

Having these options has helped me to learn what I need as I work. Assigning children to one work spot day after day doesn't give them the opportunity to learn how they work best. Children need the same tools adults do in their workplaces and creative environments.

This doesn't mean that there is one magic formula for the physical layout of the classroom. Teachers create different environments with their children to set the stage for stimulating learning. In a recent article, Sandra Lawing describes the physical environment in her classroom (Laminack and Lawing 1994). She, too, stresses that her classroom is set up in areas, not centers. She explains:

> Each area is a defined space with appropriate resources available. For example, the science area has artifacts brought in by the children: magnets, magnifying glasses, a tarantula named Charlotte, two hamsters named Bangs and Moonshine, a small plastic tub of Zoobooks, and a shelf of books sorted by topic. There are no activity cards asking the children to follow the steps, fill in the blanks, or respond to a contrived situation. Rather, the materials are available as resources and are there to be used by anyone—be it small or large groups, individuals, or partners—who find them appropriate to their inquiries. The classroom also has a functioning restaurant with posted business hours and child-generated menus reflecting recipes the children developed. There is a class bank, a publishing company, a florist in the spring, and a delivery service. There are no rows of desks, nor is there even a seat for every child to call "home." As in the world beyond the classroom, children move about the room freely and with purpose. (pp. 8–10)

Figure 2.1 shows the floor plan for Sandra Lawing's classroom.

Leslie Funkhouser creates the ability to "move about the room freely and with purpose" in her classroom, too. When I was a daily participant in her second-grade classroom, her room was set up with a variety of areas rather than centers. Over one small round table in full sunlight hung a sign: "Quiet! Genius at work." The children in Leslie's class knew this was a place they could choose to work if they didn't want to be disturbed. Other tables were pushed together in fours or in twos; several longer "lab tables" seated up to six. Beanbag chairs nestled in corners of the library area with tubs of books labeled by the children in such categories as "sport books," "mystery books," and "action books." At different times in the year, the areas included a listening center with multiple copies of children's published books and the author's recorded reading on tape; a bird feeder outside the window with pads of paper and pencils for writing observations; and a long publishing table with sufficient room to spread out covers, glue, binding materials, and labels. Organizing the classroom with areas like this shows the thought that Leslie has put into planning for the resources that children might need.

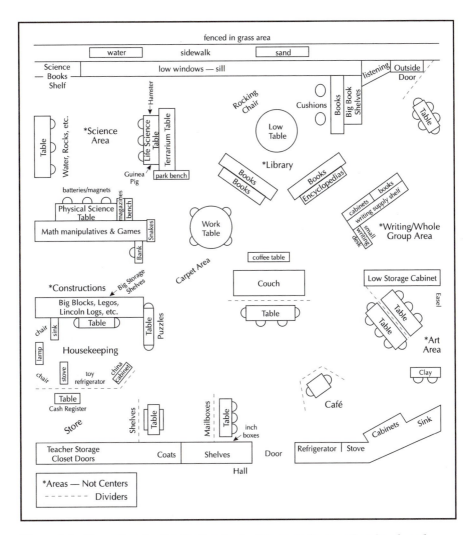

Figure 2.1   Floor plan for Sandra Lawing's classroom (source: Laminack and Lawing 1994, p. 9)

Access to Materials

Whether the areas are filled with tubs of books of many different genres or scraps of yarn and swatches of leftover material (like Pat McLure's "Beautiful Junk" bins), or crowded with the wooden blocks and building materials that grace a corner of Chris Gaudet's classroom, these areas supply not only the space but the *materials* that creative thinkers need (McLure 1987; Fueyo 1991).

Karen Ernst's "artist workshop" also reflects a respect for the kind of predictable flexibility that her students need. Like the other teachers discussed in these pages, her art classroom is set up in areas: a corner of the room for displays of the work of children and adult artists and illustrators, a gallery of mounted work for students to use as inspiration for their own ideas, long tables and round tables, files for artists' portfolios and notebooks, and, of course, art materials: paper, clay, pastels, paints, watercolors, charcoal, crayons, easels, clipboards, pads, and sketchbooks. Students need ready access to all these materials, because each artist might work with different media.

"I took status of the class," Karen writes, "asking that [my students] tell me what media they would use or the topic for their pictures. I watched with anticipation as everyone got their materials and went to work" (Ernst 1994, p. 42). Unlike many art classes, Karen has set up a structure where students are self-directed and choose what materials they need to express the ideas that they are creating. Instead of passing out supplies and leading a lesson, she describes her anticipation as she watches independent children get the materials they need for the creative work they have in mind and settle into work spaces. They are learning to build those important "houses of thought" for their work. These children are clearly not committed to the same work space and materials for the entire working time; they have the freedom to get the supplies and tools that their creative enterprises call for, as their work progresses and their ideas evolve.

Access to Other Learners

Children need specific, predictable times in the day when they can expect the chance to talk and to get feedback on their work. "When children have time to talk, they have access to a resource whose value in their lives is inestimable" (Dudley-Marling and Searle 1991, p. 135). Many theorists and teachers who advocate holistic philosophies of instruction have emphasized the importance of regularly scheduled whole-class sharing times. Nancie Atwell (1987) stresses her whole-group meetings as vital to the success of her entire literacy program and has continued to expand this concept across the curriculum in her current teaching (Atwell 1994). Donald Graves also documents the importance of children's talking with each other about their writing as a factor in their growth as writers as well as the social development of the class as a whole (Graves 1994). Literacy teachers across the country have incorporated this aspect of a writing workshop into their classes, and expanded it to include a time to share the books they are reading and their reading processes as well (Newkirk and McLure 1992; Harste, Short and Burke 1988; Ernst 1994).

Having predictable times to come together as a group—to share stories, writing, mathematical delights and dilemmas, or art—is vital to children's creative development. In a study of the Holocaust in Caryl Crowell's third-grade classroom, the daily planned discussions were essential for the children's confrontation with the reality of the historical information they were learning. The following excerpt describes a discussion that grew out of children's questions about Rose Blanche, the title character of a book they were reading, who discovers a concentration camp and returns to feed the prisoners:

> One illustration prompts several days of discussion about Rose Blanche's motivation for helping prisoners and the circumstances surrounding her eventual death. It shows Rose Blanche, with a Nazi flag in her hand, patriotically waving at a procession of soldiers through her town.
>
> Seaaria opens the conversation about this book with one of her typical questions. "How come she's waving a Nazi flag?"
>
> "That's what Travis's question was," says Aaron, who had been Travis's buddy when they read this book the day before.
>
> "'Cause right there she was waving a Nazi flag," Seaaria points to the illustration.
>
> "What do some of you think about that?" asks Caryl.
>
> "Well, I couldn't, I kind of tried to answer some of his questions but I didn't really know it either," admits Aaron.
>
> Travis suggests one explanation. "I thought that since she was German and she was waving a Nazi flag, I didn't know what was wrong, 'cause she may have pretended to be a Nazi so she wouldn't get captured that's what I thought."
>
> "Well," begins Aaron, "I think, I don't think she . . . "
>
> "Maybe they were forcing her," ponders Seaaria.
>
> "Yeah, but why would she be smiling?" asks Trevor.
>
> Aaron argues, "If they were forcing her, they would take her . . . "
>
> "To the concentration camp?" worries Seaaria.
>
> "But why would she be smiling then if she was, ya know, if she was being forced?" Trevor asks.
>
> This conversation continues for over twenty minutes. The depth of the children's unresolved questions urges them to continue the *Rose Blanche* discussion the next day. Finally, three discussion days later, Colin offers a new hypothesis for the group's consideration. "Ms. Crowell, I think one of the reasons that when she was waving that is because a lot of people didn't know that the Nazis were so mean, to the Ger, um to all those people."
>
> Travis agrees. "Yeah."
>
> Aaron also agrees calmly. "Yeah."
>
> But Trevor reacts strongly to this idea, suddenly exclaiming, "Wow! I never thought of that!" (Whitmore and Crowell 1994, p. 142)

In this example, the children show their willingness to think about issues over time, without immediately resolving their questions. It also demonstrates how children were affected and influenced by the discussions, constructing meaning from their own experiences as well as from those of the others in the group.

But besides whole-group discussions, children also need to be able to turn to another child or seek out a particular person who can be a sounding board, or who they know will give them the attention they need. Talk around the tasks can keep creative juices flowing. One afternoon, two six-year-olds in Jill Ostrow's class were working on their writing. Starla needed to talk through her ideas with Ailene as she wrote:

Excerpt from Fieldnotes, April 5, 1995

STARLA: I'm writing real small, and . . . here's what I wrote: "Once there was a African who was looking for water with her baby." *(Starla looks down at the clipboard, then over to Ailene:)* Give me some ideas.

AILENE: The mama . . .

STARLA: The mom finally found some water.

AILENE: Oh, I have the best idea in the whole world! Make the letters really big at the start. I'll show you. *(Ailene demonstrates, making a large letter at the start of the page with a fancy block around it.)*

STARLA: I'm gonna do a picture now, 'kay?

AILENE: So, how's she gonna carry the water?

STARLA: Like they do . . . um, on her head? *(Starla puts down her pencil and picks up a crayon, drawing above her writing.)*

In this short conversation, Ailene spurs Starla's thinking, collaborating by offering ideas and suggestions and asking questions. Starla feels comfortable accepting some ideas and ignoring others. This dialogue isn't simply cute classroom chatter—it sets the stage for habits that include cooperating with others in ways that can continue to nourish creative work.

One famous example of this kind of sustained collaborative effort is recorded in the letters of Albert Einstein and his lifelong friend, Marcel Grossmann. As reported by Vera John-Steiner (1985):

The two men continued correspondence when Einstein left Switzerland, and these letters allowed Einstein to test some of his ideas while they were still in a formative stage. In 1912, when the two men worked together, Grossmann provided the physicist with some important mathematical tools and thus contributed to Einstein's final formulation of his gravitational theory. Their friendship illustrates the continuing need of creative individuals to combine solitary labor with sustaining, nourishing connection with others. (p. 209)

Just like Einstein, children learn new ways to reinforce and refine their ideas and experiences when they have ready access to other thinkers. The support and thoughtful criticism of their peers can have a profound impact on their development. Transactions with others are at the center of learning environments that value the social nature of learning.

Instead of focusing solely on learning as an individual process, educators are beginning to understand the key role of collaborative learning. The social context of thinking itself is at the heart of Lev Vygotsky's influential work. Vygotsky, a Russian educator turned psychologist, conducted research that has helped childhood educators and psychologists look to real classroom spaces rather than laboratories to study children's abilities (Vygotsky 1978). His work helps us understand the ways that children transact with their world, reorganizing their understanding of concepts as they argue and negotiate their solutions to various problems. I especially appreciate his vehement defense of children as active agents in their own education. He argues for classrooms that allow just the kinds of interactions that are common in the classrooms described in this chapter, stressing that "students are capable of learning the conventions of new social contexts and new linguistic genres if the contexts are dynamic ones in which students are permitted to participate and are free to be themselves" (quoted by Goodman and Goodman 1990, p. 244). Children are able to participate most fully when they are active agents in their classroom environments.

UNDERSTANDING THE STRUCTURE

An elaborate learning structure for children will not foster their creativity if they do not understand it—and are not responsible for shaping it and keeping it going. When I visit a classroom for the first time, I often ask children to explain to me what's going on, or "what usually happens now." If kids can't tell me, it usually means they are dependent on the teacher to orchestrate all the movement in the class. They aren't able to be independent and therefore flexible in their use of time.

I remember visiting Pat McLure's class one spring morning just before the whole class gathered together in the meeting area to share their writing and reading. One of the children began to cough and cough, and it became clear that this child simply couldn't stop. Pat brought the child to the bathroom to get a drink of water and to deal with his discomfort. The class progressed with no disruption: the children gathered in the meeting area as they always did at 10:00, and the first child who had signed up to share her work read her piece, then called on students who had comments and questions for her. When Pat slipped back into the room, she sat down on the edge of the sharing circle and listened and responded as just another participant in the group. The classroom was able to run smoothly without her physical presence.

This doesn't mean that the teacher isn't important; on the contrary, the teacher has a key role in helping to set up a structure that allows the children to have responsibility for their own learning. One telling example comes from Leslie Funkhouser's second-grade classroom. As resident researcher in Leslie's room, I asked one of her students, Johanna, to give a guided tour of the classroom. We videotaped her description of the classroom areas and what went on in each area. Several themes stand out: the knowledge that Johanna and her classmates have of the structure of their classroom, their independence within that structure, and the social nature of their learning (Graves and Hansen 1986a). When I share this tape with teachers, they invariably comment on how the teacher created a structure where children know their choices and their boundaries. Though Leslie isn't the one giving the tour of the classroom, her hand is clearly present.

In Nancy Winterbourne's second-grade classroom, the children create displays to explain the structure and setup of their classroom to parents at the fall open house. The week before the evening open house, Nancy (with the help of the school's roving aide) takes pictures of all the different areas in her room, and her children sign up to mount the pictures and to write captions that explain them. Nancy takes care to make sure that each child is represented in at least one picture, and the child who is in the picture usually opts to write the description for that picture. Nancy has discovered several added benefits to this practice. Through discussion of what makes a good caption, children learn to distill the key ingredients of what sets that area or aspect of the day apart from others. The talk and writing help them internalize how their classroom is structured and how it works to promote their learning. These captions capture the flavor of her classroom community, too. There's a great photo of Nancy conferring with Abigail, one of her students. Abigail's caption begins, "Here I am telling Ms. Winterbourne a little bit about the book I'm reading." One of my favorites shows around six students engrossed in reading in the classroom library corner. There's one boy who's *not* reading, however, and he is the one who wrote the caption: "There are lots of ways to get comfortable in our library corner."

SPECIAL RULES AND EXTRAORDINARY EVENTS IN JILL OSTROW'S CLASSROOM

 In Jill Ostrow's multi-age class, the children understand the structure and procedures of their class so well that they are the experts who explain it to visitors—and to parents. At the school open house in the fall of 1994, for example, four children who had been in Jill's class the previous year explained the program and answered questions for parents. As they took turns explaining the pictures and slides depicting writing, reading, and math workshops, projects and problem work, and different areas of the classroom, they made it clear this was their room, too.

The children's personalities, interests, and needs are reflected in the organization and layout of the classroom. Cartons of books line the walls, rest in chalk trays, and spill out of tubs. The books range from wordless picture books to biographies of Jane Goodall, Margaret Mead, and Albert Einstein, from poems and fantasy books to atlases, historical fiction, and published books written by the young authors in the classroom. Soft background music fills the air, helping to create an inviting environment, with music chosen by the children from a collection that boasts, among others, Louis Armstrong (a favorite), folksinger Kate Wolf, and Mozart. The walls are covered with children's work, experiments, notes, projects, graphs, poems, and artwork. There are various places to sit and work in the room—round tables, square tables, couches and rocking chairs collected from second-hand stores or donated from friends and colleagues, and even a low coffee table with plump pillows to sit or kneel on. Children can work together or retreat to cozy corners to work alone when they wish to be undisturbed (see insert page 1).

In one corner of the room is a large "platform area" that takes up almost a quarter of the classroom space. This platform resembles two layers of connecting bleachers and serves an important meeting area (see insert page 1). The platform is a testament to the way the class has been created and built to meet the needs of the children. Two years ago, the children brought up a dilemma in one of their class discussions. The meeting area was crowded and it was difficult to see everyone during whole-group sharing time. Jill agreed and voiced her own frustration as well. In a discussion with a teaching colleague, Jill heard about platforms built in many primary schools in Italy, and she told the children about what she had learned. They decided to build a double layer of seats into the room—their own version of the Italian structure.

This turned into a long-term project. The children began by helping design the plans for what eventually became the platform area. The project started small, with the children measuring how deep the steps should be. I recall Jill's students measuring stairs and steps at home, in the community, at public facilities. They used everything from rulers to string to oatmeal boxes as units of measure. As the children refined their plans, they created a blueprint (in invented spelling), followed to the letter by a parent who volunteered to build the wooden structure. After the platform was constructed, it was clear that, to make this a comfortable and usable structure, one element was still needed: carpeting. When the children raised this issue in another class meeting, Jill turned the question back to them: How could we get carpeting to finish the platform? The children decided to write letters to local carpet stores, explaining their need and requesting remnants. Their letters show that young children can write very persuasive essays, and they got results: a company donated rug material and even came to the class and installed it, free of charge.

Though the basic layout of the classroom is fixed, it goes through tremendous changes throughout the year, depending on what the class is investigating. During the 1993–94 school year, the classroom was transformed into an island community: the children constructed life-size palm trees and an eight-foot papier-mâché mountain in the classroom. On other occasions, it's been transformed into a forest of evergreen and deciduous trees, an African village, a planetarium. In September 1994, the class built a "time travel chamber." The first trip planned was to Virginia in 1863, so in October a mural depicted a watercolor landscape of the nineteenth-century Virginia countryside. The math supplies were housed inside the child-constructed cardboard horse-drawn covered wagon, and the platform area became a country store, circa 1863. The children converted the room into what they would see as they stepped out of their time travel chamber (see the floor plan in Figure 2.2).

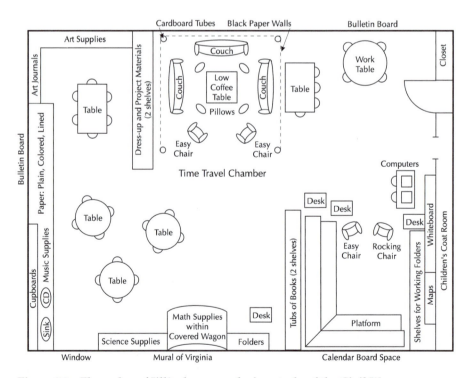

Figure 2.2   Floor plan of Jill's classroom during study of the Civil War era

As the year progressed, we traveled to other places and times, also altering the room dramatically. In January, when we traveled to the Arctic Circle, the covered wagon was dismantled and parts of it became the entrance to a snowbank, cardboard animals of the Arctic peeked from different corners of the room, and the children's questions about the Arctic hung from snowflakes and newly constructed glaciers and snowbanks (see Figures 2.3, 2.4, and 2.5).

In order for this class to work—to "travel" in time and space, and to transform itself according to the interests of the learners in the class—it must be extremely structured. Indeed, Jill Ostrow's classroom is one of the most structured and organized I have seen. It exemplifies the *flexible predictability* that is key in an environment that nurtures children's creative development. The schedule is organized around daily workshops that the children rely on: writing workshop, reading workshop, and math workshop. Predictable times are set aside for Calendar Time, for Jill's reading aloud to the class, and for the important project work the children are always involved in. The project work is usually related to the room's transformation, such as the creation of a Civil War museum, which was the culmination of the time travel trip to

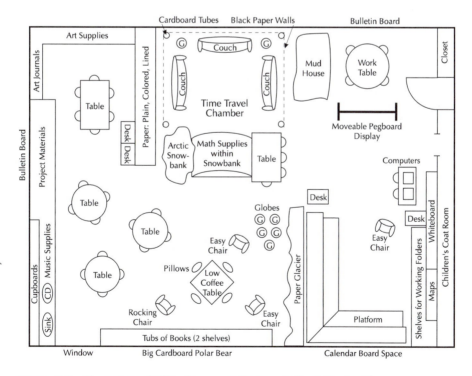

Figure 2.3   Floor plan of Jill's classroom during study of the Arctic

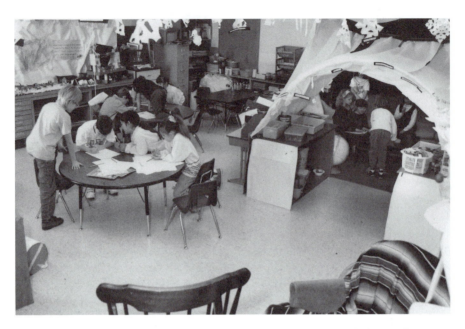

Figure 2.4 The children have ready access to materials during their travels to the Arctic.

historical Virginia, or a bridge-building project, which grew out of the island community project (see Chapter 8). (For more information on the workshops and project work in Jill's classroom, see Ostrow 1995.)

The class begins and ends each day with project work. Jill finds it provides continuity for children to end the day knowing they will be able to pick up right where they left off when they return the following morning. They typically come to the platform area first thing in the morning, often explaining to each other where they left off and filling each other in on how different groups or partners are proceeding in their work before heading off to their tasks.

The general structure looks like this:

8:45–10:15   Project work
10:15–10:30 Recess
10:30–11:30 Math workshop
11:30–12:10 Lunch
12:15–12:30 Jill reads aloud
12:30–1:00   P.E. or music
1:00–2:00   Writing workshop

Why do you get snowflakes?

Figure 2.5 The children's questions about the Arctic surround them as they conduct their research.

2:00–2:15   Recess
2:15–2:45   Reading workshop
2:45–3:15   Project work

The children's understanding of how to work flexibly within these predictable patterns is key. Because they have internalized the structure and have ready access to the materials, spaces, and people they need, these blocks of time can be juggled to make more time for longer project work or for the other strategies for learning that Jill wants to provide. Some of these are planned weekly, such as the time for art workshop or the Friday afternoon mini-classes described in Chapter 4. Some are simply part of school life—an unanticipated assembly, schoolwide testing, and the like. Other times, the culmination of a long-term project might require displacing some of the regular working times. For example, when the class was turned into a planetarium, the children took turns presenting their "star show" to other classes that signed up for the presentations. In order to make time for these shows, the regular working times were rearranged or canceled for a day or two.

The children know the expectations—the boundaries and choices—within each of these structures. When Jill was going to be out of the classroom and needed a substitute teacher for the afternoon, she knew the children could best explain the expectations for the class. In the morning, she met with the children, and they divided up responsibilities for each of the segments and wrote the schedule for the substitute teacher:

Notes for Deanne

	12:10	Pick us up from lunch
Jenna	12:10–12:30	Read to us
Joseph	12:30–12:55	We go to P.E.
Maria	12:55–1:20	We walk from P.E. to Music
Lisa	1:20–2:00	We have writing workshop
	2:00–2:10	We have recess
Stephanie	2:10–2:40	We read our books
Tara	2:35–3:00	Work on island stuff
Spencer	3:00–3:10	Clean up
Emma	3:10–3:15	Read, walk to buses

Stephanie will pass out homework folders

When visitors come to Jill's classroom, they often express amazement at the children's involvement in their work. "I can't believe six-year-olds can have such long attention spans!" one visiting teacher remarked. What these adults have witnessed is children who have entered their magic circle—their *temenos*—where they have access to the tools for creativity that they need. They have been able to create personal work spaces within a larger classroom community. This opens the door to their ability to take risks in their explorations, courting the small—and large—failures that are an essential element of the creative process.

3

Mistakes, Risks, and Challenges

Above all, there is freedom, the knowledge that you are going to make mistakes and not being afraid. To be frightened is to be in prison. By the end of that time, I was dropping mistakes right, left, and center. I learned to love making mistakes.

ANNA BRITTO

A basic characteristic of the creative process is the ability to take risks and make mistakes along the way. Researcher David Perkins emphasizes the importance of this trait when he writes, "Along with risk-taking comes acceptance of failure as part of the creative quest and the ability to learn from such failures. By working at the edge of their competence, where the possibility of failure lurks, mental risk-takers are more likely to produce creative results" (quoted in McAleer 1989, p. 47).

One of our goals, then, in sustaining an environment that encourages creativity is to help children build on their natural abilities as learners and "mental risk-takers." Think about the ways that young children acquire language—how they attempt to communicate through approximations of sounds and experiments with words, how they make creative mistakes that delight their parents and ultimately push them forward in their language abilities. This acceptance of mistakes provides a safe environment for risk taking, where failures are not punished or ridiculed, but seen as important steps along the road to learning.

A colleague told me the story of his daughter Rosemary's distress at the thought of making mistakes in school. Her first-grade class began the day with Daily Oral Language, an activity that made Rosemary afraid to speak in class, despite her exuberance in telling stories at home. The drawing she made at home shows her apprehension of the dreaded Daily Oral Language ("dale orl laweijj") (Figure 3.1). "Don't laugh at me," pleads the girl at the front of the class, and Rosemary's caption asks, "Will the girls help Lucy?" Fortunately, Rosemary's home environment allows her to feel comfortable taking the kinds of risks in her writing that will help her continue to grow in fluency. When we encourage children to stretch themselves, to work at the "edge of their competence," we also need to provide a huge safety net in the form of a supportive classroom environment.

This is built in large measure through the kinds of flexible predictability discussed in Chapter 2: for example, when Pat McLure encourages children to elaborate on their stories in their own voices and their individual ways of writing and drawing, or when Jill Ostrow builds on her children's mathematical conceptions (and gently addresses misconceptions) during whole-class mathematics shares. But there are other, more subtle elements that help weave the safety net learners need.

Jill and Pat foster an attitude of respect in their classrooms. There is a clear, underlying assumption that the children's attempts make sense and

Figure 3.1   Rosemary's written reaction to the dreaded Daily Oral Language exercise

that they are all capable thinkers. Jill and Pat not only exhibit this respectful stance themselves, but *insist* upon it for all the members of the community. Children's social skills are considered part of their working habits. Problems that arise in the way the members of the classroom treat each other are considered as serious as more traditionally academic topics. Whole-group discussions, role-plays that encourage empathy, and individual conferences to iron out specific situations are all strategies they use to help set a tone for cooperation and respect. Children expect to be treated with consideration as part of their learning; when they aren't, they have strategies for dealing with it.

When I interviewed several children about what they found difficult in their research projects about the Civil War, Starla told me that two things were hard for her: "Learning that there ever was slaves was hard," she began. "And I think how Hannah talked to Esperanza was the hardest."

"What do you mean?" I asked.

Esperanza, sitting next to Starla, explained what had happened. "Hannah was my partner, and she would say, 'Shut up,' and talk mean to me, like rude, and I don't like that."

"So what did you do?"

"I told her that I don't like that and I can't work with her when she talks that way, and if she does it again, we'll talk to Jill about it."

Creating a supportive class environment clearly isn't based on an "anything goes" philosophy; it means setting the boundaries of what's acceptable. The children have to learn that what they do and say affects the abilities of others in the class to take risks—and make mistakes.

Mistakes are, in a very real sense, the raw material of learning. If we don't make mistakes, we are unlikely to make anything at all. It is a built-in aspect of our learning process; we construct knowledge through this feeling out and trial of what works and what doesn't. In learning language, for example, children *must* risk trying out new sounds and exploring connections to different objects and actions in order to find out how they can communicate. Children's early learning environments are usually filled with this kind of risk taking, whether learning to walk, taking part in different family tasks, playing games, or forming new social relationships with other children. The risk-taking stance in learning needs to be carried over into classrooms rather than abruptly put on the shelf at eight o'clock in the morning, to be taken out again only after school hours.

Pat McLure's philosophy of children learning to write is built on her knowledge of children's acquisition of oral language: Just as young children learn to create meaning through their speech and a reinvention of language, she helps her students work out the way written language is organized so that they can "use words to create worlds of meaning" (Wells 1986, p. 156).

From the first day of school, the children write stories, using the symbols that best convey meaning for them. They use a combination of words, pictures, letters, and symbols that help them explore how to communicate on paper. Just as children's oral language becomes more conventional through experimentation, use, and the guidance of other language users around them, so does children's written language. Figure 3.2 shows the growth of Jeremy's invented spelling over the year, from capital letters representing a few sounds in September when he wrote the brief text "I HA T TE" (I had turkey) (Figure 3.2A) to his spelling of more complex words and syllables along with the use of upper- and lowercase letters in his story of the hockey game he saw in March (Figure 3.2F). (For more information on early writing programs using invented spelling, see Newkirk and Atwell 1988.)

Figure 3.2   Jeremy's writing progress, September to April of first grade. A: "I had turkey" (September). B: "I got a new lunchbox" (September). C: "Today I have soccer practice" (October). D: "Today I published my book" (January). E: "I have a loose tooth. I wiggle it a lot" (February). F: "Tonight I went to see Jeremy B. play hockey. He won his last hockey game before the championship. The score was 10 to 0" (April).

This writing philosophy causes Pat to have different "children of concern" than a teacher who sets a classroom standard of first-draft perfection. David was one child that Pat worried about. David came into class the first day of school with an oversized soccer t-shirt, a mop of tousled hair, a shy winning smile, and an eagerness to do well in school. During daily writing time, however, we seldom saw the playful, happy side of David's nature. Though he had many stories to tell, he was initially unable to share them on paper. Instead, he retreated to a reliance on the repetition of words that he could spell correctly. This limited him to the kind of meaningless stories often found in old readers, such as "The fat cat sat on a mat." Any messy erasure or clumsy letter formation would cause him to crumple up his paper, toss it away, and sigh in frustration. His perfectionism stood in the way of his ability to learn to use writing. His unwillingness to make mistakes made him unable to make stories at all.

With Pat's careful and persistent help over the year, David was able to learn to take the risks that were essential for his creative growth. Much of this was due to an environment where David saw other children's risk taking supported and nurtured. Like the other children in the class, he delighted in the stories that children read during whole-class sharing time—stories such as Sarah's, rich in experimentation and playfulness with language.

Sarah worked on her "My Pets" story for several days, weaving together the pet experiences she had had in her young lifetime. (See Figure 3.3 for the first page of Sarah's story, showing her handwriting and her placement of letters on the page.) The entire story is reproduced below, with Sarah's invented spelling on the left, and conventional spelling on the right.

I yos to hav a cat.	I used to have a cat.
hur Name was Jossufin.	Her name was Josephine.
She was a varre nise cat.	She was a very nice cat.
One nite Addran coldd	One night Adrienne called
hor u Kros the Stret	her across the street
wen a car wus ckuming.	when a car was coming.
theats the ed of Jossofin	That's the end of Josephine.
I filt like crying	I felt like crying
wen She dide.	when she died.
the next Day we wet	The next day we went
ouside She wus ded.	outside. She was dead.
frozzin stif.	Frozen stiff.
Naw i hav anuther cat.	Now I have another cat.
har Name is Muu.	Her name is Emma.
She wus a inteuLitt cat.	She was an intelligent cat.
I Dindint Noddisitel	I didn't notice until

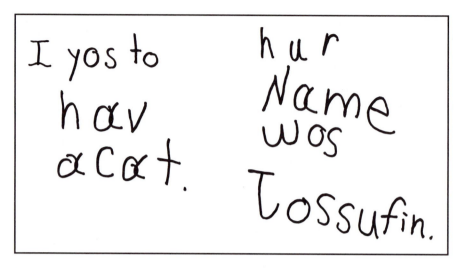

Figure 3.3   An excerpt from Sarah's story "My Pets" in her own hand

Ihed ben weth her	I had been with her
for a logtim.	for a long time.
wen I ask her sumthing	When I ask her something
She nods her hedd	she nods her head
yes or no. we hadd	yes or no. We had
to takk her uway.	to take her away.
Naw I hav a goddfish	Now I have a goldfish.
he is Name Fablet	His name is Frederick.

In this story, Sarah takes significant risks in her writing in order to get her meaning across. Rather than relying only on words she knows she can spell correctly, she reaches for the more difficult words that are part of her speaking vocabulary—words like "intelligent" and "frozen." Notice the delightful experiments that work to represent the sounds she hears in words like "Muu" (Emma) and "Noddisitel" (notice until). Taking these risks give her freedom. Sarah has the freedom to write in her own voice, with the lilt of her speaking patterns: "The next day, we went outside. She was dead. Frozen stiff." When I reread these sentences, I can hear Sarah.

And I can hear six-year-old Shauna's indignant voice when I read her "gaft" (draft) of her research report on Susan B. Anthony. The children in Jill Ostrow's class take the same kind of risks in their written research as in their personal narratives. Just three months into the school year, Shauna is fearless in her written expression and experimentation:

Siwin B ANThNE HLPT Wimn	Susan B. Anthony helped women
VRWT She Wos BoRN FiBRWiRY	vote. She was born February
15 1850 She Wos Fimis. She	15, 1850. She was famous. She
woND WimE Too VoRwT Beuos	wanted women to vote because
miN CRD uLe VoRWT She	men could already vote. She
WiNT To GiYRL Too TiMs	went to jail two times.
She Wos aRisT FoR VoWToe	She was arrested for voting.
ThAT Wos NoT RiYT She	That was not right. She
WoNT The SheRiF To	wanted the sheriff to
HaNDcoF HRe ThE SheRiF	handcuff her. The sheriff
SiD No WimiN CRD ORLeY	said no. Women could only
VORWT iN Too STiYT. Sha	vote in two states. She
TAFRLD To ORGiN iN 1905	traveled to Oregon in 1905.
She HeLP NoT GiF The mone	She helped not give the money
To The MeN She WooD NeVr	to the men. She would never
git MeRRYeD She DiYD	get married. She died
BeFoR ThE LoR PAst	before the law passed.

Shauna can devote her attention to organizing and reflecting on what she knows about Susan B. Anthony and the issue of women's rights. She can proclaim with conviction, "That was not right," and reflect with some regret that Anthony "died before the law passed." Right from the beginning, she is learning that written communication helps construct meaning.

In reflecting on my own writing process, I know I tend to write more like David than Sarah and Shauna. I'm too likely to sit at the computer, blocked because I don't yet have the perfect lead. I have experienced fear that my writing won't work; I agree with Anna Britto that "to be frightened is to be in prison." When I reflect on the writing that has been most successful for me, I know it comes from a risk-taking stance, when I "cut loose," experiment, and see what surprises are there to greet me on the page (Romano 1987). Natalie Goldberg's advice to writers has always been especially helpful to me. She tells us we *are* free—free to write the worst junk in our town, in our city, in the United States, in the universe! (Goldberg 1990). Her words remind me that I can always build on the surprises that emerge from my writing and discard the "worst junk" later—or find ways to turn it to my advantage.

Teachers, too, need to take risks. Many of the creative ideas that Jill and her children put into practice don't have a known outcome. In her story of one year in her classroom, Jill writes about experimenting with a new form of evaluation in which the whole class took notes on one another's presentations as they displayed their projects. "It was a flop," she writes, then goes on to explain the modifications they came up with based on what *didn't* work (Ostrow 1995).

These "flops" don't discourage Jill; they are simply part of her creative process as a teacher and as a learner. We all learned about the possibilities and limits of using recycled soda bottles and papier-mâché as building materials when Jill and her students plunged into creating puppets. "I don't know how this will work," Jill told the kids, "so let's give it a try. We'll meet back at the platform area in thirty minutes to talk about what strategies we've come up with that work and what problems we need to solve." A visitor in the classroom that day was amazed that Jill sent them off to work without knowing how the project would evolve. But it was clear from the children's involvement that they were comfortable with the ambiguity, and as open to learning from their mistakes as Jill.

Creative individuals sometimes discard their mistakes, but they also are open to using them, incorporating accidents into the projects they are working on. I am grateful to Jenna for introducing me to this phenomenon one day when I was interviewing her about a forest park she and a partner had designed and were now constructing. She and Stephanie were putting the finishing touches on a guided tour book to give to visitors to their model park.

Excerpt from Fieldnotes, May 19, 1993

(Jenna is pointing to a cardboard squirrel, about two inches high, placed in a clearing of the three-dimensional forest park she and Stephanie are building.)

JENNA: Now this is a statue of the squirrel.

RUTH: A statue of a squirrel . . . What an interesting idea . . . What made you decide to add a statue to your park?

JENNA: The statue was made by the Native Americans.

RUTH: Ah . . . now what made you think to put that in?

(Stephanie chuckles and looks at Jenna.)

JENNA *(matter-of-factly):*   First, I made a squirrel to put in one of the trees, but it was way too big . . . so I decided, "I'll turn it into a statue." Then I thought, "I know. I'll make it an old statue that the Native Americans made when they lived in this forest."

RUTH: Oh, so you had an accident in that it didn't come out the way you wanted it to—so you used it? You used it for something else?

JENNA: Uh-huh.

RUTH: That was a pretty happy accident.

(Stephanie and Jenna turn back to making miniature people to go on their guided tour.)

Rather than discarding her mistake, Jenna used it in her project. After my discussion with Jenna and Stephanie, I decided to follow up on what I initially termed "happy accidents" to see if they were more widespread in the class. I discovered that they were a rather natural part of the children's creative process. The following excerpts from other conversations show the kinds of "happy accidents" that the children turned to their advantage.

Interview with Spencer and Lisa

RUTH: While you were working on this project, did you have any accidents that happened that turned out to be good?

LISA *(thinks for a minute before answering):* Well, we put this fox coming out from under the bridge.

RUTH: How did you decide to do that?

LISA: Well, we just put the fox by the river first, and then we put the bridge over it and I forgot the fox was there.

SPENCER: But it actually came out to be neat, so we kept the fox where he was instead of moving it again.

Interview with Nolan

(As he explains his jungle, Nolan tells me about how he constructed a cat in his jungle tree.)

NOLAN: I knew at home that I couldn't draw the cats, or anything in the cat family, so I tried to make a jaguar, but I don't know, the only part I messed up on the cat was the face. I messed up on the face, but it looked neater when I made this guy, turning, looking at the tree.

RUTH: Oh! So let me see if I got this right, Nolan. You knew you wanted to draw something from the cat family for the jungle and you have trouble drawing cats' faces, so you experimented with it at home and you figured you could draw a pretty good jaguar, but you messed up on the face? So, when you drew it, it looked like he turned his head? So what we see here is the back of the head? I love the way you did the back of the neck—it really looks like he's turning around to look.

NOLAN: 'Cause I seen him on TV—it's that show where there's animals. They showed jaguars one time.

Interview with Kevin and Paul

(Kevin and Paul are making deciduous trees for their forest. I ask them if they had any problems as they made their forest park.)

KEVIN: Yeah! Making the deciduous trees. When I tried that, the branches didn't work out at first.

CHARLES: But I like the way they did that. It came out neat!

RUTH: Me, too. I like it, too—the branches form a kind of triangle.

PAUL: We decided they looked like rocket ships.

KEVIN: So we named them Rocket Ship Forest.

PAUL *(laughs):*   Yeah, we had a stage, though, where this tree looked like a rocket ship with a mohawk . . .

(We all laugh.)

The children opened my eyes to a kind of improvisation that grows from accidents and is sometimes beyond our control. In a risk-taking stance, a person is more likely to think, "What can I learn from this? How can I use it?" rather than, "Oh, no. Now I can't do it." In fact, Jenna defined the category with the term the children in the class came to use: "cool mess-ups."

Excerpt from Fieldnotes, September 22, 1993

JENNA *(hurrying over):*   I just got a totally cool idea from a mess-up.

RUTH: What happened?

JENNA *(showing her paper):*   I drew two kids. It wasn't looking very good, so I decided to have them turn into Tiger Girl. Then she's going to turn into something else . . . way cool. It looks like it's changing. I erased it, but I forgot that when you erase crayons, it looks like something disappearing. So I decided she would be disappearing.

Jenna was so delighted with the technique she had discovered for making a person look as if she is disappearing that she incorporated it into a detailed story about Tiger Girl. When she read her draft to the whole class, she prefaced the reading by sharing her process: "I made a really cool mistake when I was writing this story."

I knew this notion had become part of the classroom terminology when Stephanie used the term as she was drawing the bridge she was planning to construct. In her design, she drew the bridge not only from a side view, as originally planned, but also from a second perspective: an aerial view.

"What gave you the idea?" I asked.

"It was a cool mess-up, actually," Stephanie explained. "I drew a wiggly thing, and it was on the wrong side to be on the end of the clay, so I decided to make the picture be from up in the airplane. So I drew that, then I still wanted to have a side view, so I drew it from that, too."

The creative process of these children is remarkably similar to accounts of adults'. Violinist Stephen Nachmanovitch, for example, describes how he has learned to take advantage of the mistakes that affect his work:

I am playing outdoors at night, in misty hills. Romantic? Yes. But also humid. The cold and humidity take all the poop out of the bottom string, which suddenly slackens and goes out of tune. Out of tune with what? Out of tune with my pre-conceived benchmark of "in tune." I can take three approaches: I can tune it back up and pretend that nothing happened. Or, I can play the flabby string as it is, finding the new harmonies and textures it contains. A low, thick string, when it goes flabby, not only becomes lower in pitch, but because of the flabbiness will give to the bow's weight much more easily and will produce (if lightly touched) more breathy and resonant tones than a normal string. I can have a lot of fun down there in the viola's sub-tonal basement. Or I can detune it even further, until it comes into some new and interesting harmonic relation with the other strings . . . Now, I have instantly a brand new instrument with a new and different sonic shape. (Nachmanovitch 1990, p. 91)

A stance that encourages you to use your mistakes and "cool mess-ups" makes you alive to possibilities. The history of inventions is full of anecdotes like this, from Roentgen's discovery of X-rays thanks to careless handling of a photographic plate, to the phenomenon of the Post-it as a result of glue that didn't stick permanently, to the invention of the friction match:

One day in 1826, John Walker, the owner of an apothecary in Stockton-on-Tees, was in a backroom laboratory, attempting to develop a new explosive. Stirring a mixture of chemicals with a wooden stick, he noticed that a tear-shaped drop had dried to the stick's tip. To quickly remove it, he scraped the drop against the laboratory's stone floor. The stick ignited and the friction match was born in a blaze. (Panati 1987, p. 109)

But the friction match wasn't simply born at that moment; Walker had to reflect on what had happened and recognize that he had learned something from this mistake. He went on to write in his journal that the glob on the end of his stick was a mixture of antimony sulfide, potassium chlorate, gum, and starch. He then repeated the mixture and made three-inch-long matches, which he continued to experiment with, igniting them and checking the results.

This kind of mistake-making, risk-taking stance is fostered throughout classrooms that nurture children's creativity. The examples that occur are seldom as spectacular as the invention of the match or new tonal qualities, but they help create the overall atmosphere. Often it is the simple, rather mundane examples that build over time to make a rich environment:

Excerpt from Fieldnotes, September 16, 1993

(The kids are making big palm leaves out of green construction paper to put on the top of their meeting hut.)

ANDY *(looking at a big leaf he has made):* This looks more like a snake.

JILL *(to me):* I *love* him. *(to Andy)* A snake on our roof? *(She smiles and staples it to the roof.)*

SPENCER: We could have an animal on the roof—a monkey!

From this brief exchange, six-year-old Andy learns that his mistakes are not errors, that they might be seen in a new light. Instead of asking him to cut out a "better" leaf, Jill encourages his comparing it to a snake. As a result, Andy's comment sparks a whole new world of possibilities for the hut the class is building. His snake crawls across the roof of the hut; Spencer's monkey peers in at the windows; and soon parrots and flamingoes are part of the environment that surrounds the hut.

Notice how early in the year the interchange occurs. This incident shows one of the subtle ways that Jill works to create a very different working environment from the very beginning of the school year. But Jill's role is not always so subtle. She makes it clear to the children that they need to learn from mistakes as part of their process of growing more proficient at a given skill or task. Learning from mistakes is an element built into their practice—in math workshop when the children write about how they solved their problems, and in their writing time, when they are expected to edit their work, looking for words they need to correct and conventions they need to learn. Being able to recognize their patterns of mistakes help them diagnose what they are ready to learn next.

Jill also has an important, more directive role: urging her students to challenge themselves in areas that are difficult for them. These kinds of risks in thinking put learners in a different mental space—a space where the baffling and difficult aspects of one's work can be redefined as the "growing edges." To clarify this concept, consider the ecotone. An ecotone is a border between two very different environments—for example, between the shoreline vegetation and the river itself. Creatures who live in the ecotone have what is called an "edge effect": an ecotone is at the same time the most hazardous place to live and the most advantageous. Its inhabitants have to be aware of their surroundings at all times—but they also have the benefit of more choices and more varied views and possibilities.

In learning environments, I see mental ecotones—the place between what we know and what we don't know—the ideal place to be. Much like the creatures who live in the ecotone, we are forced to explore our own risky places when we inhabit this mental space. Challenge is a vital aspect of creativity—setting high expectations *and* recognizing that we'll learn from the challenges we set, even though we are courting failure.

Jill invites her learners to cross into the ecotones when she expects them to challenge themselves in their learning. In math, for example, they may not be striving for "one right answer," but they learn from a challenging experience. Instead of relying on one method or what they already do well, Jill insists that they also venture into more risky territory. In a recent math workshop, Jill issued all the children an instruction: "Do anything that will be a challenge to you." Besides submitting the work they chose to do, the children were also to reflect and write answers to two questions: "What did you do?" and "Why was it a challenge?"

The math the children chose to attempt varied from child to child. Tegan explored arrays, a kind of math that has been difficult for her. She experimented with arrays for the number 24 (see Figure 3.4). Tara, an older student, challenged herself by setting up a problem, noting that it was a challenge "because I have never made up my own problem before and usually when you do something for the first time it's challenging." As she worked through the problem she posed, she found she needed to explain, revise, and expand her problem before she could begin to try to solve it:

Excerpt from Fieldnotes, November 10, 1994

(Tara's money problem)

You have 400 dollars and you want to buy a house. Now here are the rules. You can't spend over $400. Here is all the prices of the items that you want to buy:

Couch—$30

Beds—$20

Oh, yeah. The reason the prices are so low is because you are getting them at a garage sale.

Table—$10

Lamps—$5

Mirrors—$2

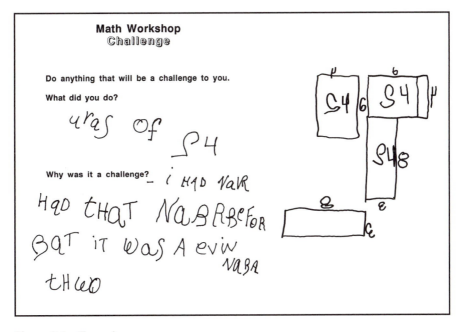

Figure 3.4   Tegan's arrays

Try to get as close as you can to $400. Now that $400 is only for the stuff that stays inside the house. It is $350 an acre and there are 10 acres of land and the house is 1050$. I want to know how much money you spend?

Figure 3.5 shows Tara's attached work.

When Jill reads the children's work, she isn't looking for a right answer. Instead, she tries to see whether the children are taking risks in their learning, challenging themselves, and adding to their learning in the process.

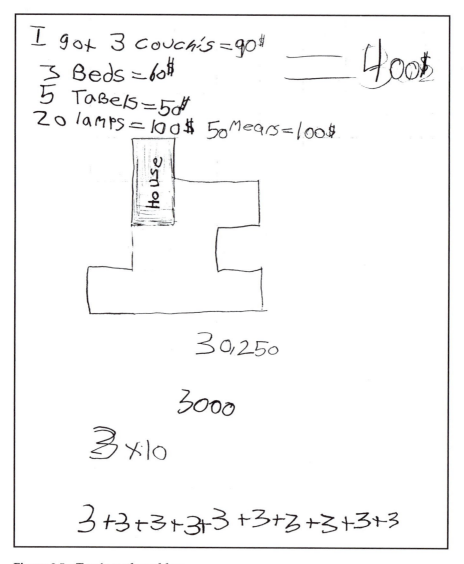

Figure 3.5   Tara's math problem

While bean problems (counting out the number of beans shaken by dice and creating patterns with the numbers) were truly a challenge for Seth, they proved not to be for Ron. Both children chose this as their challenge, but Ron found that the problem was much easier to solve than he had anticipated, and was not a challenge after all. He wrote that next time he would choose something else to challenge himself.

Rather than encouraging the flexibility, confidence, and effectiveness that grow from children's taking risks in thinking and learning, too often schools set crippling standards right from the beginning. In a recent article in *The Council Chronicle*, Kenneth Goodman argues against this trend of setting "uniform industrial standards":

> In the industrial view, schools are factories taking children as raw materials, shaping them through controlled, uniform treatments, and delivering them as "standard" products . . . In industry, it is understood that a standard is arbitrary and that things that are not standard are neither good nor bad, though they may be problematic. But as the term is used in education, the standard becomes the epitome of quality. That leads to terms like substandard and non-standard to characterize everything or everyone else. (Goodman 1994, p. 20)

Rather than setting "rigorous standards" that invite uniformity, we can help young children have high expectations for themselves and their creative enterprises by working with them to construct environments that encourage mistakes, risks, and challenges.

4

Apprenticeships

The apprentice unconsciously picks up the rules of the art, including those which are not explicitly known by the master himself.

MICHAEL POLYANI

Apprenticeship—working with a skilled mentor in a craft—is an honored tradition in most cultures. The apprentice learns more than the isolated components that make up the craft; he or she shares in the process and the passion of the mentor as well. In the kind of close collaboration that apprenticeship entails, novices see how projects start and the problems that may be encountered and solved along the way. And often the learning isn't done in isolation with the mentor alone, but in collaboration with other apprentices; peers of varying degrees of competence can help and instruct one another.

APPRENTICESHIP AS A NATURAL LEARNING STYLE

 Apprenticeship is the most natural form of learning. We are apprentices to language competence from the moment we are born. The way young children learn language in the home is a clear example of being apprenticed to the more skilled language users that surround them. It is not passive learning: babies are not subjected to a series of isolated skills. Instead, they are surrounded by language being used in context, and they begin to participate in it, gaining more and more experience in the craft of conversation. We learn language in order to participate in conversations, to take part in what people around us are actively doing. In his classic study of language learning, *The Meaning Makers* (1986), Gordon Wells stresses the importance of talking to learn as a key component of learning to talk:

> Children love to help with jobs that their parents are engaged in. When they are allowed to help, these shared activities can provide particularly rich opportunities to learn—about the activities themselves and about the words by which to refer and also the way in which language functions to guide action. (p. 53)

In the home, children witness parents through direct observation and through taking part in activities with them. Wells gives examples familiar to families in Bristol, England—of young children taking part in daily cooking activities, or learning the steps involved in preparing clothes for washing. The children begin by observing and starting to make sense of the daily activities that surround them, then they participate to a greater and greater degree. This informal learning is similar to the weaving apprenticeships of young Zinacanteco Indian girls in Chiapas, Mexico:

> Young girls first gain familiarity with weaving by watching their mothers at work. Later they help boil the threads and dye the wool. At about the age of eight, they make their first serious effort to learn to weave. The mother initially provides considerable guidance, a mix of talking and demonstrating. But as the child gains facility, the overt instruction diminishes, until by the age of 11 or 12, the pre-adolescent girl is able to proceed pretty much on her own. (Childs and Greenfield 1980, p. 179)

Learning in this and all apprenticeships is contextualized; by "hanging around" and being part of the swirl of daily life, children are apprenticed to other skills and languages for learning. In this atmosphere of building naturally on children's abilities, no one sets out to break down the complex, interrelated use of language, tools, and interaction into a set of discrete, isolated skills to be learned out of context in a lockstep fashion.

In his book *Diary of an Artist* (1977), Raphael Soyer describes the process of learning to draw in his home as a social process. Soyer's father, a poet and artist himself, was constantly drawing, from "pictures of Cossacks on horses with all the trimmings" to life drawings of family members. Raphael and his twin brother, Moses, picked up the tools that littered their environment and learned to draw in the same kind of informal apprenticeship as the young weavers from Chiapas, or the children learning to cook in Bristol.

These novices learn from direct observation, from experience, from talk—from being surrounded by a craft and learning from others who have more experience. They are nurtured by the personal attention of the adults they work with, the lively conversations that are part of their tasks, and the real-world application of the skills they are learning.

When children enter schools, or places organized for more formal learning, we can build on what we know about the importance of the apprenticeships as a way of learning and expanding children's creative abilities.

TEACHERS AS MENTORS

 In the classrooms I have observed and worked in, the teachers see themselves as members of the larger community but also as important mentors to their students. One of the key elements of successful informal apprenticeships is the active role the mentors take—in making and doing as well as in instructing. Though this should be an obvious first step, it is one that is often ignored. In writing classes in the past, for example, it has been far too common for teachers to assign writing, yet never practice the craft themselves. When teachers write and share how they write with their students, they are able to provide more than the overt activities that make up the skill of writing—they can share their own inner processes as well.

Nancy Winterbourne invites her second-grade students into her composing process right from the start. Early in September, the children had paired off to share the writing they were working on with a partner when Nancy called them to the meeting area. In her lap was a stack of drafts of writing she had worked on. She wanted to take this opportunity to talk to the children about her writing process, as well as her expectations for theirs.

Excerpt from Fieldnotes, September 12, 1989

NANCY: I've got a rough draft and a final draft up here. Now remember, we're making a bulletin board for the first graders about buses. That will be a final draft for the bulletin board. When you're getting ready to publish and put it in the hallway, it's good thinking and good handwriting. A final draft is your very best. Your journals, though, can be a rough draft when you're thinking your ideas out still. (*She holds up a copy of a typed letter to parents.*) This is a letter I wrote to go home. It looks pretty good, huh? This is how it started out (*she shows the messy first draft, Figure 4.1*). This is the second draft (*holding up another page, handwritten, but with fewer crossouts and lines than the first draft*) that I gave to Mrs. Peters to read. And this is my final typed one (*Figure 4.2*). Which do you think is the most important to me?

KIDS (*various responses*):   Final draft . . . the last one . . .

NANCY: Not to me. The rough one is the most important. The *ideas* are here. You have to get the ideas out of your head and here onto paper. You can see this was hard work. Writing and reading and thinking go together like this (*clasps hands together*). I want you to get to final drafts, but you have to get your ideas out on paper first—and share those ideas with friends, like I did

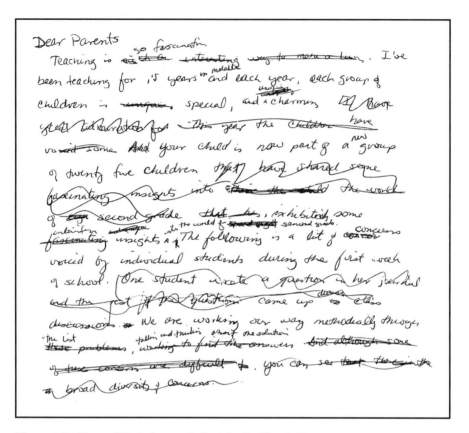

Figure 4.1   Nancy Winterbourne's first draft of her letter

with Mrs. Peters. Ruth and I share our writing back and forth all the time, too. OK, we've got twenty minutes left before recess. Let's turn to our reading. How many of you have already chosen a book to read?

In this brief discussion with the children, Nancy shows her students her working process—not just her creative and imaginative process, but how literacy fits into her daily life as a teacher. She doesn't talk down to her students, but uses the terminology of writing naturally. She also demonstrates that she is writing for a real audience—in this case, the children's parents. By doing this, she invites her students to use the writing workshop time in their class in similar ways: for genuine purposes of thinking and communication.

The children in Jill Ostrow's class know she is a teacher researcher who makes sense of what happens in the classroom through her notes, journal writing, and narratives. They often hear drafts of these writings, as well as the poems, stories, and other pieces of writing Jill is working on, at whole-class sharing times. When she wrote a narrative about what she learned through a

September 1989

Dear Parents,

Teaching is fascinating. I've been teaching fifteen years in Molalla and each year, each group of children is special and uniquely charming. Your child is now part of a new group of twenty-five second graders offering some interesting insights into their childhood world. The following is a list of concerns, questions, and problems voiced by individual students during the first week of school. The students and I are working our way methodically through the list, talking and thinking about the solutions.

- Someone put their hands around someone else's neck in the bathroom.
- There are too many kids for one teacher to love.
- When will we get our reading books?
- When will we learn cursive?
- The journal covers are too dark and some journals have plain pages and some have graph paper.
- When will we get playtime in the classroom?
- The box to carry the lunchpails was very full.
- What about homework?
- What about tattling?
- When can we work in our math books?
- What about hurt feelings?
- What can we do when we feel left out, when we feel we are not loved?
- What should we do when we see something that is against the rules?
- What can we do if we are scared or worried at school?
- My mom forgot to have me practice reading.
- When are we going to study dinosaurs?
- Someone was grabbing at lunch tickets, someone was slapping back.

I have asked the children to talk and share ideas with one another, to make consensus decisions, to be and to agree on what is polite. I have asked the students to make choices on material to play with, material to read, partners to work with. I have observed the interaction, the abilities of individuals to focus and concentrate on a task, the willingness and skills in cooperating and also levels of energy and fatigue.

I am looking forward to calling each family during the next two weeks. We can discuss any specific concerns or questions you may have and I can share some of my observations. I can be reached at the Primary School from 8:00 to 8:20, 11:45 to 12:00, and 2:15 to 3:45. Please feel free to call me at any of those times, as your schedule permits, and if it's more convenient than a call from me.

Yours truly,

Nancy Winterbourne

Figure 4.2   Nancy's final, typed letter

writing conference with Micah, she shared it first with Micah himself, and then with the whole class, asking for their reactions and input. When the piece was published in *Teacher Research Journal* (Ostrow 1994), the children were excited to see the final published product, especially because they knew the steps that had led to it—the drafts, revisions, and galley proofs. Unlike other children who have not been intimately involved in the process, these kids know that published writing doesn't emerge with first-draft perfection. Whether it's fiction, poetry, letter writing, drawing, mapmaking, research, or musical composition, teachers who share their processes invite their students into a more meaningful apprenticeship in the crafts they practice.

There are important benefits for teachers as well as students, too, as art teacher Bill Childs writes: "Even as I am a teacher of art, I can't imagine not being an artist and a student as well. Certainly as I work, I am reminded of the challenges, frustrations, and achievements that are experienced by my students. As it is important to feel a sense of satisfaction through the growth of my students, it is important for me to feel that I am achieving something on a more personal level as well" (quoted in Rief 1992, p. 3). The excitement that Bill feels as he explores his craft with his students isn't just the icing on the cake—it's a vital aspect of the role of mentor, igniting the passions of students.

Karen Ernst found that in her artists workshop, her behavior as an artist and writer had enormous influence on her students' learning: "In our artists workshop, students observed my inquiry as an artist as I worked on my own pictures and collages or sketched them while they worked. They would find me writing in my journal if they came to the art room early in the morning or if they noticed me sitting outside while they played on the playground during recess . . . The opportunity to participate as apprentices in the artists workshop enabled my students to learn and interpret in many ways" (Ernst 1994, p. 81).

These apprenticeships also provide the learner with insights into the actual steps involved, the tools that are available, and how to use those tools, as well as the more hidden inner processes of thought. Novices can learn what mentors have forgotten that they automatically do.

OTHER ADULTS AS MENTORS

 In interviews with the children in Jill's classroom, I discovered that they have learned a great deal from the adults in the room in just such unconscious ways. Jenna surprised me by commenting, "Well, I've learned a lot of stuff from *you*. I picked up a habit from you. Now I write notes all over stuff. You have that habit."

Jill verified that Jenna "picked up this habit" and showed me fieldnotes that Jenna had taken on other children in the class. Jenna spent a recent writing workshop observing her classmates as they worked. Her fieldnotes on Tara show her eye for detail, and her tendency to write in the present tense, recording what is unfolding around her:

Jenna's Fieldnotes, October 1994

Tara: She's writing, concentrating. She has 1 leg under the table. Now she has both. She is talking to Shauna She is reading her story. Micah says something to her. Now, Carl has too. She is reading her story to all of them. Now Micah and Carl leave. Tara is still reading her story to Shauna She now has no legs under the table. She is playing with her pencil on her shirt. Shauna is helping her get ideas.

Jenna also honed her research skills by observing me, as I talked with children in the room, as these fieldnotes show:

> *Ruth:* She is listening to Fiona and Molly share. She is listening very intently but not recording it. She is admiring Fiona's little braid thingey and saying she used to have one, too. Now she has come over to me and Jill tells her not to. Now she has left the room with Alice Cotton [fifth-grade teacher].

Jenna was observing me long before she picked up her pencil and began to take fieldnotes. Because I have been a member of the class for three years, my research activities have been woven into the fabric of the class in more ways than I had imagined. Other adults who interact on a regular basis have acted as mentors for different skills in other surprising ways. Maria commented that she learned from Cherry, "the one who comes in and works with Ben sometimes. I've learned from her how to calm Ben down."

Cherry's unruffled, caring presence in the classroom has taught the children ways to work with Ben and, beyond that, has set a model for how to interact with children who need extra support in the classroom. One of the key elements of a successful mentor relationship is the personal interest of a caring, interested adult, even if it is in an informal, rather than structured, way.

Just as we can be mentors within the class, we can also foster other apprenticeships by inviting other adults from the community into the class. Some might be short-term mentors who come into the class to share their passion and expertise on a particular topic. For example, during the study of the Civil War, Jill invited a historian who specializes in Civil War reenactments. His influence built on Daniel's interest in clothing from the Civil War, who haunted second-hand stores with his mother to put together his own "authentic" Civil War outfit. Many other adults have played mentorship roles in the classroom, such as Kathy, Daniel's mom, who met weekly with a small group of children to explore life stories; Rob, who worked with the children on the long-term project of building the platform they designed; and Mike, the animation artist who conducted small-group classes after school for students who were interested, worked with children through class demonstrations, and made himself available to individual students who wanted to take their animation work further, into three-dimensional work through claymation.

Some of the adult mentorships came about through Jill's deliberate planning and a desire to build on the skills of people in the community; others emerged naturally and were encouraged to continue. Over the course of three years, photographer and videographer Jim Whitney documented the learning in the class, making visits an average of three times per year. At the very first visit, seven-year-old Nolan was fascinated not only with the equipment but also with the entire process of the shoot. He followed Jim as he worked, asking questions and watching closely. Building on Nolan's interest, Jim invited him to be his unofficial assistant, taking the Polaroid pictures that helped determine if the light settings were correct. During writing workshop later that week, Nolan wrote a letter to Jim to thank him for the experience (Nolan's own words are at left; conventional spelling is at right):

to jim from nolan	To Jim, from Nolan
thak you jim for asre all the kawhin tath I askt at you nowe it was variy fan takh you varye varye mahe for latn me takhe pakhrs and lating me payl lthe paprhe salmhe aprt it was vare fan take you for taking tim off of wat you ware doing it take me a varye laghe tim to do all tis raiting	Thank you, Jim, for answering all the questions that I asked you. You know it was very fun. Thank you very very much for letting me take pictures and letting me pull the paper slimey apart. It was very fun. Thank you for taking time off of what you were doing. It took me a very long time to do all this writing.
by jim	Bye, Jim.

Indeed, writing was a slow and often difficult process for Nolan, and Jill was delighted at this genuine communication, which was longer and more detailed than his usual work. The picture that he attached to the letter also showed how carefully he had observed and noted details of the equipment (see Figure 4.3). The fluorescent lights, which run the length of the ceiling, figure prominently in Nolan's picture, as Jim had complained of how this typical form of school lighting affects the way the images are recorded on camera. Nolan also drew the lens cap hanging from the camera, the prominent eyepiece, the top and side camera grips. Interestingly, he added what look almost like rays coming out of the video camera, imagining the view of the room captured by the lens.

From that initial experience, Nolan became Jim's photographer's assistant, taking on more and more responsibility with each shoot. In March 1995, Nolan, no longer a member of Jill's class, received permission from his fourth-grade teacher to work for the day in Jill's room when Jim came once again to document the images and learning as Jill's students explored the Arctic. The first thing Nolan did when he greeted Jim early that morning was to pull out a stack of recent photos he had taken at home, going through each one, talking about what worked and what didn't. Two photographers discussing their craft.

Figure 4.3   Nolan's picture of photographer Jim Whitney at work

As I eavesdropped on their conversation as the day progressed, I was amazed at how much Nolan had learned over the past few years.

"OK, Nolan, when Seth's dad comes in for the portfolio conference, where do you think would be the best place for them to sit, since we're taking these pictures without extra lights and with black-and-white film?"

"By the window, I think, 'cause of the natural light?"

"That's what I think. Why don't you go over by the table and take a light reading with the meter?"

When Nolan read the meter, he screeched his surprise: "Wow! Jim, can you remember the very first time you got a reading this high?" Throughout the day, Nolan continued to experiment with the light meter, predicting readings as he measured the darkest corners of the Time Travel Chamber or the pools of light flooding through the window.

"Nolan, you're a real master with that meter!" I exclaimed at the end of the day, as we were packing up equipment.

His smile reflected his pride in accomplishment. "At first, I was just clickin' it. But now, I'm usin' it like I've known how to do it forever!" He looked up at Jim hopefully. "It would be neat if I could go around with you on other shoots . . ."

"It sure would, Nolan. We'll see what we can work out this summer."

Apprenticeships like this, even when they are separated by stretches of weeks and months, can still have a profound impact on young learners. Nolan knows his questions are taken seriously, as he plunges into a complex process with a combination of hands-on learning and observation. Perhaps most important, he has the attention and respect of a caring adult. Experiences like this don't have to take place only outside of school; they can be braided into learning as part of the school day. There will be different roles for adults, and different niches within the school year, but we can all work to find and build important mentor relationships for our students.

CHILDREN AS MENTORS

In collaborating with others, we round up as in any relationship, an enlarged self, a more versatile creativity.

STEPHEN NACHMANOVITCH

It isn't only adults in the school and in the community who can serve as mentors. Although the dominant classroom structure in schools continues to be either teachers at the front of the classroom lecturing to passive students or students working individually on seatwork, more and more learner-centered classrooms are built around the concept of students interacting, working in pairs or small groups in the context of social learning. In classrooms that encourage such "collaborative-apprenticeship learning," the peer interaction has been found to encourage significant cognitive development in students' abilities to analyze, evaluate, and speculate on alternative viewpoints (Bayer 1990; Bruner 1987; Forman and Cazden 1985).

According to Lev Vygotsky (1978), the novice's boundaries lie between what she or he can do independently and what she or he can do while participating with more capable others. He calls this the *zone of proximal development*. This influential concept is the cornerstone of educational theory built on a social, interactive perspective. Vygotsky stresses that it is when learners engage in joint activities that the concepts they are grappling with are best developed. According to his theory, "an expert (or more knowledgeable peer) initially guides a learner's (novice) activity; gradually, the two begin to share problem-solving functions, with the novice taking the initiative and the expert peer correcting and guiding when she or he falters. Finally, the expert peer cedes control and acts as a supportive audience" (Brown and Ferrara 1985, p. 83).

Multi-age classrooms such as Jill Ostrow's are particularly well suited to this kind of collaborative-apprenticeship learning. Raised on this way of learning, the kids can articulate how it benefits them all (see insert page 2):

Excerpt from Fieldnotes, February 22, 1995

RUTH: What's different working in a class with kids who are six, seven, eight, nine years old? All those different ages . . .

MARIA: It's fun. Really fun.

JULIA: You learn from older people because it's sort of like they've been in the class more so they can teach you more about stuff you've never done.

MARIA: And some of my ideas I get from first graders for stories. For projects . . .

JENNA: Like Taylor. Take Taylor. She is so good at coming up with totally goony, harebrained ideas for stuff, and that is so cool that she can be independent and this is her first year in the class.

RUTH: Now, when you were in first grade, there were older kids here. Do you remember which of those kids you learned from?

JENNA: All of them.

RUTH: All of them. Can you think of an example of a time you learned something from somebody?

JENNA: Well, what was it . . . Paul was doing something, and I went up to him, and I'm like, "How do you do that?" and he showed me how.

RUTH *(to Maria):* You used to work with Paul a lot. Do you remember anything he used to teach you, or what it was like to work with him?

MARIA: Well, he was fun to work with because . . . remember the frog pond problem? That, it was really fun to work with him and he was my partner.

JENNA: He shares jokes, too.

MARIA: Paul, he was the only one who could read my writing when I was in first grade.

In multi-age classrooms like Jill's, children seek out the more experienced learners in the class who can help them in their learning. Maria and Jenna, two older children, also appreciate the value of learning from children who are younger than they are. They can get wonderful ideas for writing and for projects from first graders like Taylor, for example. They also remember how they learned from older children who acted as genuine mentors for them, as Paul did for Maria.

There are also structures built into the class so that all the children have a chance to act as mentors within a more formal teaching stance.

Mini-classes

Every Friday afternoon, the children look forward to their mini-classes. In these thirty-minute classes, five or six children volunteer to teach something to a small group of their classmates. They know they will be responsible for planning, teaching, and reflecting on these mini-classes, and they take this responsibility quite seriously. They are the mentors in this apprenticeship situation.

Each Wednesday, Jill calls for volunteers who want to teach on Friday. The activities they teach range from executing karate kicks in the gym to drawing Civil War figures to creating geometric math patterns. Some classes are so popular that they need to be repeated; Micah's briefcases were such a hit that he needed to teach his mini-class over and over until every member of the class (including Jill and me) had his or her own poster-board and duct-tape carrying case. At other times, a mini-class might not be conducted because of lack of interest by members of the class.

Mini-classes allow everyone to share a particular strength or something they have recently learned that they'd like to pass on. First graders teach these mini-classes as often as third graders, getting the chance to explain their craft or skill to an appreciative audience that has signed up to learn from them.

The mini-classes have been so successful that Jill recently added them to her math workshop. On Wednesdays, during math workshop, children sign up to conduct math mini-classes. The children who teach these mini-classes sit at a table and work with a group of other children for ten minutes, then another group comes to them, until they have taught three or four groups. As with the Friday mini-classes, these math mini-classes vary greatly. On one particular Wednesday, I sat in the following groups:

- Molly helping children solve problems using the orange cubes.
- Daniel teaching an "Arctic animals" game, assigning values to the different geometric shapes that the children used to create patterns of animals.
- Maria teaching place value through trading in chips.
- Tegan teaching a pattern game with unifix cubes.

At the end of math workshop, Jill called all the children to the platform area and asked them, "What did you learn today that you didn't know before?"

Jeremy began by calling out, "I learned a new game! I'll want to play it again in math workshop."

"Sure," Jill responded. "The classes you are taking now you can explore more on other math workshop days."

"Oh, good!" exclaimed Taylor. "'Cause I learned a fraction game."

"Well, I added up higher numbers than I ever have before," Ron told us.

"Me, too," Kelly chimed in. "I used the orange cubes all the way up to hundreds mats."

First grader Hannah was also excited to share her learning: "I used the chips, and when I got five whites, then I gotted one red. I never traded before."

Maria, her teacher for the trading, added her comment to the discussion as well: "Yeah, she did real good at this!"

Apprenticeships Between Classes

Discussions of what the students learn in their role as teachers demonstrate that the older children benefit as much as the younger ones from the experience. Many teachers experiment with this kind of cross-age tutoring when they don't have the benefit of many ages in one class. Second-grade teacher Leslie Funkhouser instituted a program where her students signed up to work with the kindergarten children in Florence Damon's class during writing and reading workshops. Leslie explained to me that the children "adopted" a kindergarten child to help with either their reading or their writing. "One day a week for about fifteen minutes they work with this child. My students are responsible for planning what they will do, keeping their appointment, and sharing with their classmates how it went. So far, their comments have been very enthusiastic and they think it's great."

When I sat in on a class discussion of the teaching, I too was impressed with these young teachers. Just reading a transcript of one of their debriefing sessions, a reader might easily mistake them for interns in a teacher education program, as they seriously discuss issues of teaching and learning.

Excerpt from Fieldnotes, March 3, 1985

"I'm working with Andrea," explains Emily. "She's shy but very nice. The first time she didn't want to read, so I read a book to her. Then this week, Mrs. Damon asked her to read from her writing to me. Their books aren't like ours—they're just learning words and mostly put down letters. Lots of their stories don't have titles, either. But Andrea can spell and read 'cat' and 'dog.'"

"What will you do next week, Emily?" asks Heather.

"I'll bring a book to read to Andrea, but I don't want to push her yet."

Leslie follows up on Emily's comment, asking, "When do you think a teacher should push, Emily?"

"Well, it will take a while. She needs to get used to me. Then maybe we can make a book together of pictures or things she knows. I think she knows 'ball,' too. Do you think I should spell words for her? Like if she drew a ball and she only knew B, should I tell her a-l-l?"

"What do you think?" Leslie asks.

"Maybe I should talk it over with Mrs. Damon."

"Lisa is shy, too," Alisha explains with more excitement than she usually shows. "She wrote about rainbows twice and shared her stories with me. She likes rainbows a lot. So do I, so we may write a story together about them."

"Were her stories the same or different?" asks Jamie.

"They were a little different but had some colors the same," Alisha explains.

"I had some problems. I don't have enough to do for the whole fifteen minutes," says Andy. "Also, David doesn't want to do what I tell him. I said we should pick out a book to read together, but he didn't want to. I don't think I did very well with him today."

"Why don't you bring David to our room next week, Andy, and I'll help you both work it out."

Leslie's role in this cross-age program is vital. She talks through the problems with the children, and shares their delight in their successes. She is also enthusiastic about the knowledge her kids are showing they have internalized about the process of literacy learning.

"I visited Florence's classroom to check on how things were going," Leslie told me, "and Josh explained the work he was doing with Daniel. 'We're reading over Daniel's stories to think of other topics he can write about. He wants me to help him make a topic list. Before it's time to go, I want to have him get two or three topics down in his book. Then he'll have more ideas for stories.' Isn't it extraordinary? I'm so impressed to hear the sophisticated decisions they are making about what the little kids need, and how to work with them."

The learning goes both ways, as the confidence of the older child builds. Michael, who struggled with reading, returned to the classroom positively beaming. "I was excellent!" he told his classmates. "I read two books, *Tim* and *Al*, to Sevey and she really liked them. I didn't miss any words, either!" Nate echoed these sentiments when he talked about his work with Jerry. "I didn't realize how good I was at reading and writing until I helped teach Jerry. I've got tons better this year!"

From colleagues in the classroom to children down the hall or across town, we can help create opportunities for a range of apprenticeships.

Group Collaborative Apprenticeships in Action

Besides classroom structures where one child acts as the mentor for one or more other children, cooperative group situations are another important way to foster informal collaborative apprenticeships. Group apprenticeships occur daily in Jill's class as the children work on long-term projects. As a kind of case study, the Arctic Adventure project demonstrates how this kind of apprenticeship can be woven into the structure of the classroom.

From January through March of 1995, when the children's "adventure problem" focused on the Arctic, the class was organized into partners and groups that crossed ages. In order to prepare for their "trip" to the Arctic Circle, they first returned to the multi-age work groups they had formed at the start of the year as part of their year-long time travel projects.

The lawmaker group, for example, reviewed the class laws and presented their suggested changes to the class for a vote. Tara (age eight) and Carl (age seven) included Ron (age six) in their discussion about why it might make sense to delete two of the laws. It was Ron who acted as spokesperson, reading the rules they had rewritten, while Tara explained, "We thought we could take away two of the school rules because everyone knows them now: no running in the hall, and that we need hall passes." Simply by being a part of these working groups that keep the class functioning, the younger children learn how the classroom works and what their rights and responsibilities will be as part of this classroom community.

As the children plunged into their Arctic Adventure project, they worked in more structured collaborative-apprenticeship partnerships. Jill organized the adventure and asked children to choose a person of a different age to work with. Tara, a third grader, chose six-year old Griffith as a partner. Tara began by reading the "Arctic Journey" problem aloud to Griffith, then together they examined one of the class globes to find where the Arctic Circle is and what countries are part of it. Griffith was able to help find the countries with Tara's guidance, relying on her experience using maps and globes. Together, they discussed which three countries they would choose to visit as part of their adventure, what they would buy to bring with them on their trip, and how they would set up their budget. (Figure 4.4 shows their completed "Arctic Journey" page.) Their journey notebook shows how they alternated keeping records, Tara doing one page, then Griffith filling out the next (see Griffith's "budget sheet" in Figure 4.5 and Tara's map of their route in Figure 4.6). This strategy continued as they composed their diary entries for the trip. First they would discuss their daily adventures, then they would take turns writing them down (see their joint entry for January 20, 1995, in Figure 4.7).

A week into the adventure, Jill instructed the groups to "take a rest at the nearest town" (see Figure 4.8, which presents Jill's printed instructions and Tara and Griffith's responses). Griffith and Tara decided to build a large model of their town in the corner of the room, changing the problem to square feet from square inches as they worked on a 3-D "authentic" mud house. The hands-on component of this part of the adventure helped make

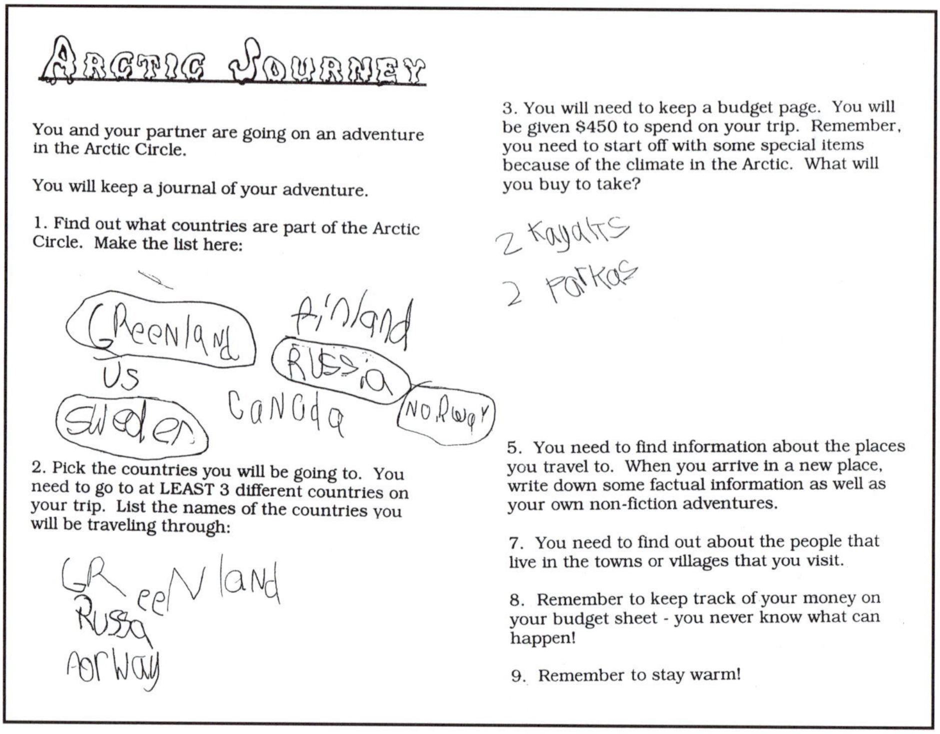

Arctic Journey

You and your partner are going on an adventure in the Arctic Circle.

You will keep a journal of your adventure.

1. Find out what countries are part of the Arctic Circle. Make the list here:

Greenland Finland US Russia Sweden Canada Norway

2. Pick the countries you will be going to. You need to go to at LEAST 3 different countries on your trip. List the names of the countries you will be traveling through:

Greenland
Russia
Norway

3. You will need to keep a budget page. You will be given $450 to spend on your trip. Remember, you need to start off with some special items because of the climate in the Arctic. What will you buy to take?

2 Kayaks
2 Parkas

5. You need to find information about the places you travel to. When you arrive in a new place, write down some factual information as well as your own non-fiction adventures.

7. You need to find out about the people that live in the towns or villages that you visit.

8. Remember to keep track of your money on your budget sheet - you never know what can happen!

9. Remember to stay warm!

Figure 4.4 Tara and Griffith's "Arctic Journey" problem

new concepts such as base and perimeter more concrete for Griffith; he was able to work within his zone of proximal development. It also helped Tara reinforce her knowledge of these mathematical constructs. By explaining them to Griffith and finding ways to explore them herself, Tara's own understanding deepened and will more easily be transferred to other contexts.

Besides the adventure problem, the children collaborated as they researched the questions they had brainstormed about the Arctic. Their questions hung from every available space in the room, from the sides of the time travel chamber to the snowflakes the children constructed (see Figure 2.5). They included such questions as:

How do animals survive?
Why is there a midnight sun?
Why are there polar bears instead of regular bears?
What kind of plants are there?
What do the people eat?
What are the birds called?
Is there more summer or winter?

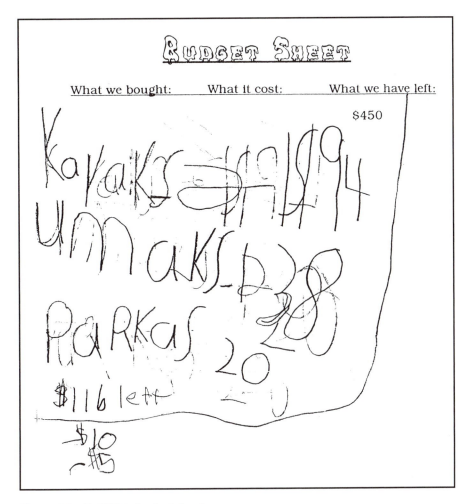

Figure 4.5   Griffith's budget sheet

How low can the temperature get?
How do they make stuff?
How do they make fires when it is so cold?

The children organized themselves into different, larger multi-age groups for researching the answers to these questions. Jenna listed me as an "alter-nite officer" in their research group, which consisted of Jenna (third grade), Julia and Carl (second grade), and Esperanza (first grade). This research was a genuine collaboration that involved all the children, from the brainstorming of questions to the editing of the final reports. Though it would have been easier for Jenna, the designated group leader, to simply go through the

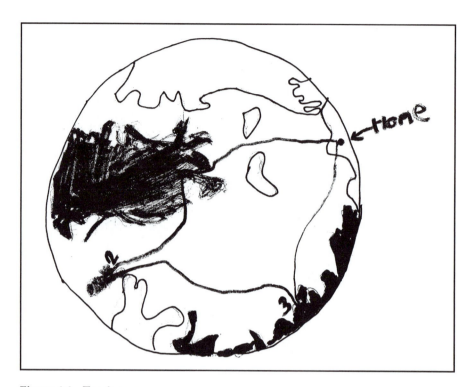

Figure 4.6   Tara's map

report and correct the work of all four children, she took her role of leader seriously, orchestrating the editing process and choosing aspects of the writing on which to base mini-lessons. Some of the report she read aloud, inviting her team members to make the necessary changes. "What can we do?" Jenna asked the group. "This says 'surviv.' What do we want it to say?"

"Survive!" Esperanza called out.

"Add an *e* on the end," Carl instructed.

Julia wrote in the *e*, and Jenna read the next paragraph, waiting for the others to suggest changes, and sometimes posing questions to the group as they proceeded. All the members of the group contributed to the final report, which became part of the classroom resources on Arctic information.

Besides books, pictures, class readings, and a trip to a local Arctic museum, the children also relied on native experts. With the aid of technology, they engaged in a kind of "cyberspace apprenticeship" with sixth-grade children from Alaska. Jill established a correspondence through e-mail with Terri Austin's sixth-grade class in Fairbanks, Alaska. Terri's older students shared their firsthand knowledge and experience with the travelers from Oregon.

Figure 4.7   Tara and Griffith's joint Arctic Journey diary entries

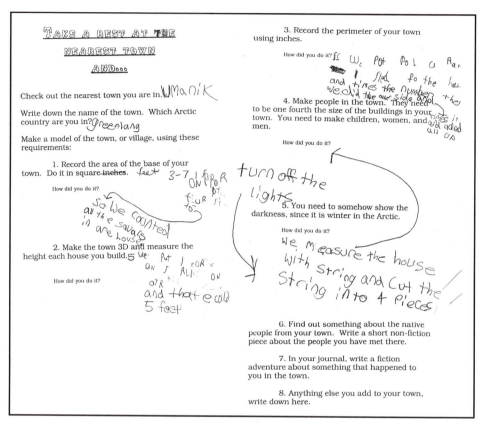

Figure 4.8   Tara and Griffith "take a rest at the nearest town"

This study of the Arctic is only one example of how the daily fabric of the class is based on collaborative apprenticeships, as older and younger children benefit from being in an atmosphere of learners who are at different stages of learning, yet who are all immersed in the tasks at hand.

THE IMPORTANCE OF DISTANT TEACHERS

Learners can also be apprenticed to "distant teachers"—mentors separated from them in time or location. Cellist Pablo Casals claims his greatest teacher was Bach, and throughout his life he began each morning playing Bach's fugues and preludes. Similarly, students in classrooms learn from mentors as diverse as Henri Matisse and S. E. Hinton. Pat McLure tells the story of one of her first-grade students approaching her with a recently completed collage and saying "I'm just a little Ezra Jack Keats, aren't I?" (McLure 1987).

Distant teachers have been important mentors for me at different stages in my creative life. As an art student, I admired the works of Georgia O'Keeffe; I emulated her close-ups of flowers and experimented with her bold use of color. Though I never worked with her in person, she became a genuine mentor to me through her works and her writings. I also recall a particular breakthrough in my drawing, when I learned a technical skill from the Renaissance artist Raphael. Assigned to do thirty pages of bones in my sketchbook, I struggled to give more energy to my tight pencil drawings. I spent hours hunched over my notebook, laboring from my corner in the anatomy lab. Later that evening, looking through pages from Raphael's sketchbook, I saw that, rather than drawing exactly from nature, as I was trying to do, he played with the light, bringing a vibrancy even to lifeless bones. His charcoal and pencil drawings had darkened accents at each joint, which created a tension in his drawings that mine lacked. I still remember the excitement I felt as I worked late into the night with my soft lead pencil, shading the knuckle, wrist, knee, and ankle joints, putting into practice a skill I had learned from a long-dead teacher.

Surrounding students with the works and words of artists, historians, scientists, mathematicians, musicians, writers—creative people from the past and the present—can help them find the distant teachers who can be important mentors for their learning beyond the classroom. Karen Ernst documented the many times that her students learned from the artists whose works she brought to her classroom studio. "Students were inspired and influenced by these artists as they chose their own topics and learned techniques at their own pace. The works and words of these artists provided a means for students to think, see, model technique, and open their imagination" (Ernst 1994, p. 84). Part of our role as teachers is to help students find their distant teachers; without access to a wide range of resources, they may not connect with the kinds of creative thinkers that can help guide their thinking.

When Jill uses her limited classroom funds to buy books and other resources, she looks for biographies and autobiographies that will connect to the lives and interests of her students. Knowing Maria's fascination with chimps, for example, prompted Jill to search out children's biographies of Jane Goodall. Jenna and Micah's interest in invention led Jill to purchase books on Thomas Edison and Albert Einstein. Through the year, the children conducted research on their distant teachers: Stephanie studied Margaret Meade; Micah explored the life and work of Einstein; and Tara read everything she could on Elizabeth Blackwell, the first woman physician. I was delighted, of course, to find a kindred spirit in first grader Fiona, who was as

enthralled as I am with the work of Georgia O'Keeffe. Together we read stories from O'Keeffe's childhood, and we both discovered parallels to our own
processes as artists. Fiona particularly loved the stories from Georgia's childhood, where she got into trouble at school for drawing what was important
to her rather than what the teacher insisted she draw.

Howard Gardner (1991) believes that incorporating apprenticeships into
schools is the best way to build on children's creative learning abilities. The
stories from the classrooms I have researched that incorporate a variety of
informal apprenticeships support this belief. In such an atmosphere, children learn skills as needed and, most important, *in context* rather than when
the syllabus or the district sequence of skills requires. Apprenticeships make
connections between the tools of the trade that help the craft and the different phases of the creative process. Children learn to use whatever tools they
need as the task requires. And since they are learning these strategies on
their own terms, they naturally incorporate new technical language into
their vocabulary and invent new terms when necessary to describe their
process. They can rely on drawing, writing, gestures—whatever tools will
aid them as they work. And they experiment with how to use these tools as
part of their apprenticeships. Most important, they take joy in this immersion in learning, incorporating the important dimension of play into their
creative work.

5

Playfulness

Creative work is play; it is free speculation using the materials of one's chosen form. The creative mind plays with the objects it loves. Artists play with color and space. Musicians play with sound and silence. Eros plays with lovers. Gods play with the universe. Children play with everything they can get their hands on.

STEPHEN NACHMANOVITCH

Taking unbridled delight in the doing, immersing ourselves in joyful expression in the here and now; allowing our minds to take flight, imagining and testing out possibilities. Playing is a kind of experimentation, a way of stretching the boundaries without thinking about either rewards or punishment. The pleasure of the doing itself—the process—is the goal when we play. Reports by creative thinkers emphasize their immersion from early childhood in the playful aspects of their crafts. Einstein wrote of playing with a compass for hours on end; filmmaker Ingmar Bergman vividly recalled operating a toy "magic chimney" that repeated films of dancing light on walls; linguist Noam Chomsky played with language and delighted in word games. "Learning, playful learning, an interest in learning and exploration that characterizes so many gifted individuals may contribute to the fluency and ease in the work of some creative individuals," Vera John-Steiner (1985) concludes. "The flow of words, of visual associations, of musical themes, of scientific ideas, which are first experienced in the context of childhood wonder and games, [gives] support to mature individuals when struggling with the more complex aspects of their craft" (p. 41).

Creative thinkers' reflections abound in these experiences. Unfortunately, these biographical accounts also highlight the extremes between the playfulness they were able to engage in informally and the spartan structures of their formal schooling. Though taking joy in our learning is one of the most important aspects of creativity, it is seldom discussed as a goal in today's schools. Most schools continue to differentiate sharply between "work" and "play" even as early as kindergarten. But in a classroom workshop rich in creative possibilities, playfulness is encouraged and fostered.

Play has important implications in children's development. Vygotsky (1978) discusses the key role of play in activating the zone of proximal development:

> Play creates a zone of proximal development of the child. In play, a child always behaves beyond his average age, above his daily behavior; in play, it is as though he were a head taller than himself. As in the focus of a magnifying glass, play contains all developmental tendencies in a condensed form and is itself a major source of development. (p. 102)

As I watch children in classrooms grapple with problems, take risks in their thinking, engage in complex and creative problem solving, I find again and again the importance of play in their processes. In fact, play is often at the heart of their experimentation. As she worked on planning and building a bridge with Jenna, Maria created an elaborate story-world that she incorporated into the design, with props of water, boats, and people to run the boats.

"The boat is gonna be so big," Maria held up her hands to show me the size of the imagined boat. "So we put straws on the bottom so the people don't fall in the water. When the people fall in, they'll get cold 'cause the water's so cold—and, um, when they get real cold, they'll be froze for, like, 'til they get in their car and stay there and put the warm stuff on. Then they can sail back through."

Maria continued to move her paper people out of the water and back to the boat as she talked. "So this can be a ferry sometimes, up to the bridge. And the cars can go on and wait until they get to the other side."

"So what is it you're building while you tell me this story?"

"I'm building a boat, see, and it goes through the bridge. And plus, when the boat goes through, you pull the pin up—then you hook the pin back through." She demonstrated how, when the boat approaches the pin and straw bridge, the bridge lifts to allow the boat she has built to go through. "It's kinda hard to put it back . . . but sometimes bridges *do* do that."

She continued to experiment with making the bridge go up and down, then decided to modify her story. "But these boats are gonna be so tiny that they can fit right through."

I tried putting one of the new, smaller boats through the waterway. "So the bridge won't have to lift and go back down again?"

"Yeah," Maria nodded. "And the cars can go on top."

As she creates a story, imagining people getting wet and cold and wanting to ferry across the water or go under the bridge in tiny boats, Maria is toying with possibilities for the construction of the bridge. She is immersed in the here and now, yet playing allows her to find new insights and possibilities in her thinking. She seems "a head taller than herself," as Vygotsky would say, because she is acting as if she is already competent in her endeavors; she has an all-important ownership in the direction of her activities.

Children like Maria, who learn to be playful as part of their learning process, bring that to their future learning situations. In his landmark study of the possibilities of play, *Playgrounds of Our Minds* (1980), John Barell found that the richer our play as children, the more likely we will become playful adolescents and adults. He describes this trait of playfulness as being characterized by a sense of humor, manifest joy, and spontaneity in social, physical, and intellectual domains. "As a result of their many different ways of having fun, [playful adolescents] appear to be very flexible in their approach to life—they exercise their ability to transcend immediate social, emotional, physical, or intellectual situations and make something else out of them. This flexibility, I believe, is crucial to becoming healthy, adaptable adults who are in control of their lives" (p. 7). A body of work by anthropologists supports Barell's assertions; play as improvisation, they have found, sharpens the human capacity for dealing with a changing world (Miller 1973).

Humorous playfulness adds pure enjoyment to our endeavors. Can you think of times that you were willing to devote time and energy into jokes, hoaxes, or play rituals? This time can feel energizing because it takes you away from more mundane or stressful problems that you might be dealing with. Recently, I had the chance to hear Mozart's "Musical Joke," a piece he wrote when he was involved with solving the problems of his darkest opera, *Don Giovanni*. This musical jest is an elaborate piece that combines the typical errors made by an inexperienced composer, "from wrong notes and other pratfalls to more subtle structural errors designed to amuse other professionals" (Oregon Symphony Program Notes, April 5, 1995, p. 32). Playing with this musical joke allowed Mozart to recapture his enjoyment in his craft, and he viewed his musical play as important in his life as his more serious operatic work.

I also recall an elaborate playful experience I took part in with the help and collusion of the office staff at Lewis and Clark College, where I teach. A couple of years ago, in the midst of our busiest time, admitting new students and going over their files, several of us spent inordinate amounts of time putting together an entire application file for Barbie. At first it was an informal office joke that Barbie was entering the Nineties and needed a career—why not come to Lewis and Clark Graduate School? Over a few weeks, though, it evolved into giving Barbie a full name (Barbara Joy Mattella), transcripts and a college major (Leisure Studies), and an interest in becoming a physics teacher. By the time we had decided to have Barbie apply as a science intern, we had delegated people to write letters of reference, a résumé, and the flood of detailed information that is required for application to graduate school. It's hard to remember how I made time to write Barbie's essay and fill out her application by hand (circling each *i* instead of dotting it). Though it was totally "useless," the time I spent on this play activity energized the other aspects of my work. And to the credit of my colleagues who read Barbie's file "blind," they good-naturedly accepted her into the program—conditionally; after all, they reasoned in her acceptance letter, she should prove to be "a model student."

Like other play experiences, my work on Barbie's application existed more for the doing than the done, more for the sheer pleasure of the experience itself than the punch line of the final acceptance letter. Play is its own reward. In play, we learn about ourselves, explore the unknown, and create new realities.

In classrooms that nurture creativity, teachers make spaces for playfulness, helping children incorporate the flexibility and adaptability that is so crucial to creating novel thought. These spaces are embedded within the structure of the class, the schedule of the day, and the philosophies of the teachers across a range of curricular areas. And they build on children's natural strengths and abilities.

LANGUAGE, LITERACY, AND PLAY

 Children play with language from a very early age. In discussing children's oral language acquisition, Bruner (1984) argued that "children's language use is . . . most daring and most advanced when it is used in a playful setting" (p. 196). When children imagine themselves making dinner, flying an airplane, or being a superhero, they try on different language patterns than the ones they normally might use, and even invent new ones in the midst of their play. It is a joyful experience of creative play where they are able to be in charge, directing the process of discovery and invention.

Children often turn to writing with the same kind of pleasure when they are in control of the process—when they are able to write and draw on topics of their choosing, and bring the elements of their imagining and play worlds onto the page. For example, in Nancy Winterbourne's class, on the first day of school, Ryan wrote, drew, and created a new reality as he playfully imagined a superbus hero.

 Maria works in a quiet nook of the room.

 Jill and a group of children work in the platform area during math workshop.

Eight-year-old Lisa and six-year-old Fiona work together during writing workshop.

The island community meets in their partially constructed meeting hut.

 The "time travel chamber" leads the children into their imagined worlds.

 Esperanza shows the reflection of the fire on her face.

 The children work on their bridge designs.

Jill confers with the children as they explain how they are solving their construction problems.

Excerpt from Fieldnotes, September 5, 1989

(I sit next to Ryan as he cuts an edge off a paper bus he has drawn.)

RUTH: Can you tell me what you're working on now?

RYAN: I'm cutting this extra line out where the wheels are. And these are the wings in the bus. I put an *S* for Superbus. This wheel is up front. This is the bus driver. Since my bus is so tall, I was thinking that it would be in the middle. I put the kids up here. So that's also sort of why I did the tail. The bus came out too tall for the stairs to go up.

Ryan is creating a cohesive reality on his page. He begins with the contours of the bus and draws the people in it near the top of the bus, not as he has experienced with his "real" bus. Instead of drawing the bus as a representation of the one he rides, he struggles to make his own bus "work." The tail of the bus swings the children up, because going up the stairs would be too much for the little children in the bus the way he's represented it.

As Ryan continues to work, he alternates between labeling his story with letters (*B* for bus, *F* for fire) and drawing and pasting elements of the superbus story to the page. He cuts out more strips of paper to attach to the end of the bus, explaining, "That's the pipe with the fire coming out 'cause it's going so fast."

"So you've noticed that in your bus?"

"No, I have little toy cars at home with sparks coming out of the back. I'm gonna color it red to look like fire."

Ryan brings his play with toy cars at home into his play at school. He knows it is safe to continue his explorations on the page, so he uses symbolism (red representing fire) and creativity as he cuts out streams of exhaust-fire to attach to his superbus. The writing works hand in hand with the visual image of the bus, as Ryan pushes himself forward, using letters to help reinforce what is happening in his imagined story.

In the field of emergent literacy, research into the importance of play is well documented by researchers such as Strickland and Morrow (1989) and Power (1992). Children play with conventions of texts, chapter headings, "about the author" pages; they also play with how language looks on the page, trying different forms of handwriting, colors, spatial arrangement of words. One child in Pat McLure's class even did a page of writing where each letter on the page was a pop-up.

Play in literacy acquisition helps children manipulate meanings, take risks with materials and conventions, use the writing as a kind of extension of their usual play. Stories and drawings of Ninja Turtles and Power Rangers may be the bane of elementary teachers' writing programs, but they serve a purpose for the children in their early explorations. Beyond fantasy, children also use writing to project themselves into more realistic situations, such as their being teachers, acrobats, firefighters, or parents.

Juliet, in her story "When I Grow Up," projects herself into the role of an adult. She is quite specific in what her imagined adulthood will look like:

Figure 5.1   Juliet's illustration

When I grow up, I want to be a story writer and a artist. I want a yard fence. If I had a picked fence, and a tall fence, it would be easier for my kids to open., and they would climb the fence. I just want two kids. I want a girl and a boy. I want to name them Tony and Krissy. I want to marrie sombody that is very strong because of all the drug dealing, and the drunk people and the croocks. I want lots of pets. I want a blue house with a white roof. I want a nice flowerbed. I am 8 and 1/2. I will get married when I am 20 or 24. I want a big garden every year. I want a sidewalk write in the middle of my yard. I want my sidewalk to go strate and then turn onto the steps and then there is the door and the porch. I want my porch to stay nice. I want to milk my own cows. I want two cats. I want six dogs. I want twenty horses. I want one goat. I want my own waterbed. I want my own horse. I want my own chair that nobody else can sit in. Same with my husband and kids. I want an upstairs, too. My kids will not be spoiled. The End.

Figure 5.1 shows Juliet's drawing of how she imagines herself with her future family.

Juliet pours her fears and hopes into her writing, imagining how she will deal with things that frustrate or scare her by having a fenced-in yard and a strong partner to keep her safe. She imagines space of her own, both in terms of a garden and her special chair that will be off-limits to everyone else, including "husband and kids." By projecting herself into the future in her play, she is able to take on new roles and perspectives.

CREATING NEW WORLDS

To play is to participate in an event that takes place by chance, entails risk, and is of remarkable import; it is to have an adventure.

ROBERT NEALE

 One of the most important attributes of play is the "let's pretend" aspect involved in having an adventure. Children imagine themselves in other roles and create elaborate mental worlds and play spaces to match them, using whatever props might be handy to enhance the situations that evolve from their play.

In Jill's class, creating new contexts—whole new worlds within the four walls of their schoolroom—is an essential component of the curriculum itself. The year that the students created an island community (1993–1994), they first immersed themselves in building that play world, experimenting and stretching themselves as they worked. They built palm trees, a central meeting hut, and a variety of props around the room to add realism to their island. Daniel, for example, explained an anchor he had built. As I entered the class one morning, I noticed that Daniel was hooking a brown paper anchor attached to a rope onto the doorknob.

"I thought that if we didn't have an anchor, we'd float away," Daniel explained. "The anchor is attached to the ship. Every morning, I come in and attach the anchor to the island."

"How'd you decide to do it?"

"I was thinking about an anchor for the boat, and then I just thought of it, and I got a rope from Jill."

As the children constructed their island world, they took on the role of shipwrecked sailors. They wrote a story about their trials at sea and what happened after they arrived on their island. After a morning's work of creating the island environment, they met at the partially constructed "meeting hut" in the middle of the room to share what they had built so far. (See insert page 2.)

LISA: We've been working on the hut.

JILL: What kind of hut?

SETH: A meeting hut out of grass and palm leaves.

JILL: Why not oak leaves?

CHARLES: 'Cause this is a tropical island! There's no oak trees here!

NOLAN: Also, palm leaves are better because they're bigger than oak leaves.

The conversation continued as a combination of story-weaving, problem posing, and planning:

Excerpt from Fieldnotes, September 16, 1993

MARIA: And there was a storm and a palm tree came crashing down on our roof.

JILL: Oh! What did we do?

TEGAN: We patched it with more palm leaves.

ANDY: I'll do more leaves!

LISA: And Stephanie and me are building an info center.

JILL: What's that?

STEPHANIE: Where you put out information about what we know about the island. It's a two-woman one.

JILL: What's next?

FIONA: We need coconuts to eat.

JILL: Yes, we need to eat.

KEVIN: We could get a coconut and make three holes, put water in it, strain the salt out so we could drink it.

JON: We could fish.

SETH: You wouldn't really find chairs on an island. Maybe we should make them rocks, cover them with paper.

DANIEL: Maybe we need an airplane with a rescue sign overhead.

MARIA: I'm gonna make a person to put on the door. She's gonna be saying, "Welcome to our island."

As the children left the meeting area, Charles told Seth to be careful on the blue rug, which was now a "blue lagoon." "Hold your breath!" he warned as he "swam" through the water, pulling his arms over his head in a swimming motion. Then, he pointed worriedly to my feet. "Don't step in it!" he exclaimed. "Put your feet up on the platform so they won't get wet."

The children's reliance on imagination in this new situation is essential in helping them generate novel thought. They are transcending their immediate reality, thinking, acting, and feeling their way into something they have never experienced, imagining what is not present. Jill gives them the choices that they need in this play situation: the children act with freedom, interest, and control over their own destinies. Jill is not outside of the play world, though; she remains open to the magic of imagination and play with them, helping them structure the environment as a backdrop to their learning.

But much of the role-playing that occurs in the classroom is more structured. For example, after the island lawmaker group created laws governing the island community, Jill encouraged the children to act out what would happen if someone broke the laws. They role-played imaginary situations and created a court system that decided how to handle infractions. As in many play situations, the children brought their knowledge of law from the larger culture into their role-plays, calling individuals prosecutors or defendants, making objections, and threatening to clear the court. But within this play were genuine engagements with the "what ifs" that might occur in such a situation and the reasons for the laws that had been framed.

The island premise provided a perfect backdrop for the creation of an imaginary world and an exploration of the need for people to explore decision making together as they create communities. But the island was only one such vehicle. The following year, we created a time machine and traveled to various times and places, and my fieldnotes from that year are brimming with examples of similar creativity, from building the time travel chamber itself to imagining a variety of worlds and places, from the

South during the Civil War to the Arctic Circle to the United States two hundred years in the future (see insert page 3). During the fall excursion to Virginia in 1863 alone, the children created the following adventures that combined play with immersion in different worlds and roles within those worlds:

- The children prepared debates between Confederate soldiers and Union soldiers that were audiotaped and heard by other classes.
- They mapped escape routes and detailed plans for a family's escape through the underground railroad.
- Each child conducted and wrote an imaginary interview with a child from the Civil War period.
- The whole class engaged in "what if" conversations around such ideas as: "What if Lincoln hadn't been assassinated?" and "What if the South had won the war?"
- The children presented plays using the clothing of the period and exploring such issues as emancipation and the women's suffrage movement.

During these and other activities over the year, the children used play to encourage their ability to think in innovative ways. Jill used their imaginations as a springboard for directing the curriculum; they learned that their play could lead to discovery and wonder. In a natural progression to the pleasure of research, they learned to use books, pictures, newpapers, and experts as resources to help them further their expanding notions. They played with language and increased their vocabulary and verbal flexibility and fluency; they played with each other as they solved problems and stretched their abilities to compromise and see other points of view; they played "what if this happened to me" and became more empathetic to others' experiences.

John Barell (1980) highlights the importance of "Playing What-If" in developing children's skills as historians:

> By playing with time, place, action, and character students become aware that the events of history closely resemble those in their own lives. Because history is a search for understanding or meaning, and meaning is revealed through connection, relations and associations, teachers can establish links between Salem witches or the pioneers of the Old West and today's students. History can be revealed not as a discipline about past events that must be memorized and regurgitated, but as a continuous process of establishing linkages of meaning within the past and between the past and the present . . . Students will then perceive themselves as "history makers," decision makers with futures created from as many options as they can imagine. (p. 43)

ADVENTURES IN MATHEMATICS

 Mathematics need not be the serious and somber study of numbers and formulas that it has been for so many of us. Play in math can be a natural part of the day, as it is in Jill's class, when the children come up with their fractions of the day or ways to make the day's date (see Chapter 2). Susan Ohanian's book *Garbage Pizza, Patchwork Quilts, and Math Magic* (1993) brims with examples of classrooms where children play with numbers and create riddles and adventures with patterns and manipulatives. She reports on Nancy Litton's group of first- and second-grade students who published their own mathematical riddle book:

> Their favorite riddles have to do with multiples and exhibit their thinking about multiplication (not standard fare for first graders). Nobody is telling these children to memorize $2 \times 4 = 8$; they are enjoying figuring it out on their own—and challenging their classmates with this problem:
> What has 8 legs, 4 eyes, and 1 mane?
> A lion and a lioness. (p. 229)

Like the children in Nancy Litton's class, Jill's students delight in challenging each other with figuring out multiples and designing problems and mathematical adventures to play with. During the study of the Arctic, they designed explorations and wrote problems for children in a first-grade class in their school, problems they thought would be fun to solve. Rather than memorizing tables, they challenge each other to think in terms of multiples.

For example, six-year-old Tegan wrote this problem:

A snowflake has 6 sides, so how many sides do:
  3   have?
  5   have?
  7   have?
  10   have?
Explain how you solved it.

Six-year-old Travis solved the problem, as shown in Figure 5.2.

Carl, age seven, came up with another snowflake problem:

Design a Snowflake

It's going to be look like this:
   It will have 6 sides. And 6 sticks coming out of each side. And it should have on top of each stick 1 circle with the same snowflake inside it. 1/3 should be blue, and the rest should be white.
      How did you do it?   What does it look like?

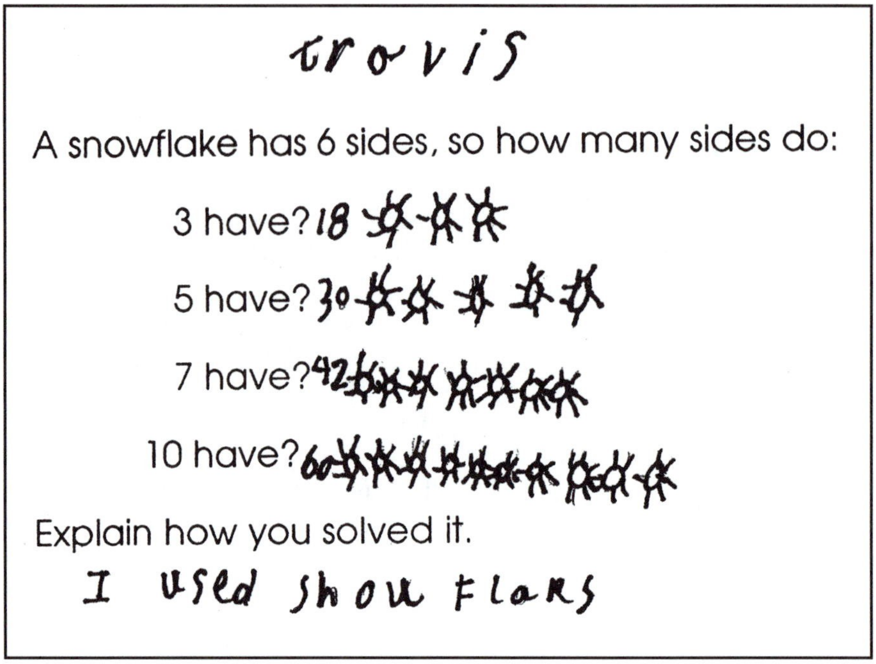

---

travis

A snowflake has 6 sides, so how many sides do:

3 have? *18*

5 have? *30*

7 have? *42*

10 have? *60*

Explain how you solved it.

I used show flars

Figure 5.2   Tegan's snowflake problem, as solved by Travis

Six-year-old Sue solved Carl's problem, as shown in Figure 5.3.

Both Tegan and Carl ask their respondents about the process: how they did it is as interesting to them as the end result.

Explorations in math are also woven into the larger real-world problems that the children solve, and they know they have the freedom to play imaginatively with budgets and money. In the "Holiday Party Problem," for example (Figure 5.4), the children created an imaginary party that required play money and a real budget. Lisa and Stephanie decided to have a country and Western party and proceeded to play store, creating a fold-out "reseat" (receipt). They included marketing ploys such as "value size" and "mega! sale!" items. They also played with the numbers so that the total of their purchases came to exactly their $50.00 limit (see Figure 5.5). Micah, Joseph, and Isaac planned a basketball party, to which they invited Michael Jordan, Clyde Drexler, Terry Porter, and other basketball heroes. Their budget page shows the food they imagined they would need as well as the cost of their

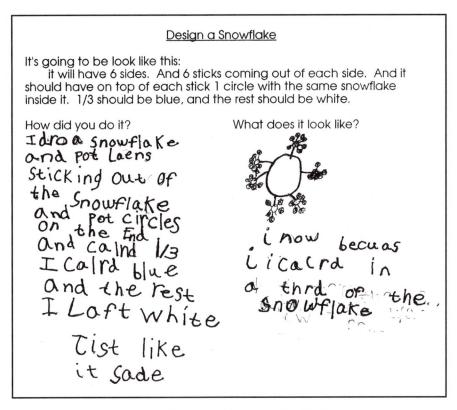

Figure 5.3   Carl's snowflake design problem, as solved by Sue

supplies and decorations. Jon and Paul had the most fun playing with the money itself; they tell their story through physical representations of the currency. "We started with . . ." their story begins, with a drawing of a fifty-dollar bill, and progresses through their purchases, until they spend their last two dollars on balloons.

In other problems, children play with geometric shapes, extending their abilities to hypothesize "what would happen if . . ." In their designs of gardens, ponds, and forests (described in Ostrow 1995), children rearranged parts of rectangles, generating alternative ways to represent square units. Though this is challenging work, it is also playful—the children have control over the direction of their work, they imagine and take risks and, most important, they know it is the process, not the "answer," that is important.

HOLIDAY PARTY PROBLEM

You have $50.00 to spend on a holiday party for a group of 6 friends.
You must:
  • Spend as close to $50.00 as you can.
  • Have the following at your party:
    • 2 different kinds of snacks.
    • a dessert of some kind.
    • decorations.
    • something for each of the 6 friends to take with them at the end.
I want to know:
  • What you spent your money on.
  • How much *each* item was.
  • How many of each item you bought.
  • What the total bill was.
  • What change you got back.
Ideas and hints:
  No item can cost more than $5 and no item can cost less than $1.
  You may want to look in the paper for some actual prices.
Other stuff:
  Make the actual money you spent. (Make the dollars and coins.)
  Draw a picture of your party and include all of the stuff you drew.
  Describe the holiday party you had.
  Put it all together in a book.

Figure 5.4   Holiday Party problem

A FEW WORDS ABOUT EXTRINSIC MOTIVATORS

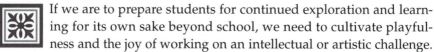 If we are to prepare students for continued exploration and learning for its own sake beyond school, we need to cultivate playfulness and the joy of working on an intellectual or artistic challenge. Unfortunately, extrinsic motivators, such as grades or rewards, actually undermine students' intrinsic motivation (Lepper, Greene, and Nisbett 1973; Kohn 1993). In play, we respond creatively to tasks we enjoy *for their own sake*, not for an extrinsic reward. Adults who love their work clearly do a better job than people who are putting in their time only for their pay. Why should it be different for children? When they enjoy and are interested in their learning, they are far more likely to learn.

Children have a fundamental desire to make sense of their world. They typically come to school with curiosity, asking questions ceaselessly, playing with language, numbers, and ideas. In the creative classes in which I have worked the children are neither graded nor rewarded with stickers or tokens. They build on their interests and questions, have a degree of control in their learning, and are important members of their own evaluation teams. Their natural, intrinsic motivation to learn is supported and expanded, not deadened by exposure to grades and an endless quest for outside motivation.

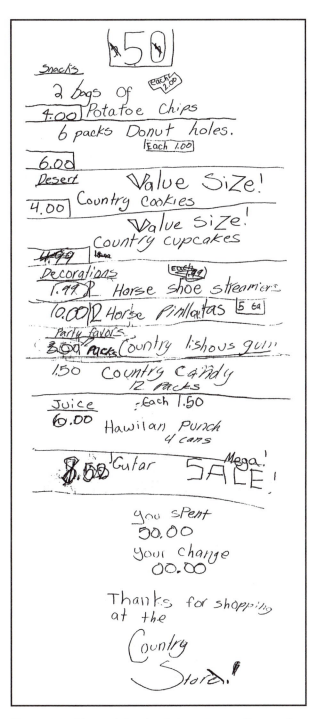

Figure 5.5 Lisa and Stephanie's party supplies receipt

John Dewey's words ring as true today as they did eighty years ago:

> If there is not an inherent attracting power in the material, then . . . the teacher will either attempt to surround the material with foreign attractiveness, making a bid or offering a bribe for attention by "making the lesson interesting": or else will resort to low marks, threats of non-promotion, staying after school . . . But the attention thus gained always remains dependent upon something external. True, reflective attention, on the other hand always involves judging, reasoning, deliberation; it means that the child has a *question of his own* and is actively engaged in seeking and selecting relevant material with which to answer it. (1915, p. 198)

Rather than perceiving their teachers as the dispensers of knowledge who hand out information, grades, and rewards, children can learn from teachers as mentors in the classroom. And instead of seeing their classmates as competitors vying for grades, they can experience what it means to play, experiment, and learn together in a collaborative environment.

Exceptional experiences in learning are possible for children when their classrooms contain the ingredients that nurture their creativity. The next three chapters present a close-up look at what is going on in children's minds as they think and create in workshop communities. What is possible for children in their invisible mental workshop?

6

"And Memory Raining Down"

I have everything I need. A square of sky, a piece of stone, a page, a pen, and memory raining down on me.

HARRIET DOERR

Memory: In our best creative moments, it rains down on us. Sometimes those brilliant, clear flashbulb memories light up our inner landscapes and beg to be recorded. At other times we sit with eyes closed, trying to nudge the details of an encounter—a time, a place, a tune, a conversation—out of the corners of our minds and onto paper. Memory is the invisible tool that writers, artists, mathematicians, and scientists rely on in their creative endeavors; it is the key element that comes up again and again when artists discuss how they create, from Mozart's references to reaching into his "bag of memories" in order to compose to Toni Morrison's vivid descriptions of her memories as the "subsoil" of her work.

Yet when we turn to schoolchildren, to helping them develop the tools they need to create, the references to memory suddenly disappear. The most common image of the role of memory in school has tended to be that of a cobwebbed storage vault, with certain items being stored in "long-term" memory and others waiting in the wings, ready to be spit out of "short-term" memory onto tests and into oblivion. It's time we take a fresh look at the role of memory, in learning and in making meaning. It is an important invisible tool for children as they hone their creative minds.

A BLUEPRINT FOR MEMORY

One morning during reading workshop time in Nancy Winter-bourne's classroom, seven-year-old Jolene talked with me as she read a book about a birthday party. I had asked her to tell me about the book, and she responded with memories of her own birthday party. This discussion led to her speculating about how your head can possibly hold all those memories:

Excerpt from Fieldnotes, February 1, 1990

JOLENE: [The book] was making me picture my birthday party because, um, my mom and dad won't let me go in my room and see what my new presents were.

RUTH: So the picture and the story that you made in your mind from reading wasn't really about what you read so much as about your own story about your birthday?

JOLENE: And it made me think of this one birthday party I went to. My mom says I can remember everything. It's weird because you have a whole bunch of memory and, you know, if you could remember everything, your head would have to be *this* big! But it's not!

RUTH: You do have a big memory!

JOLENE: I know, it's really weird. I wonder . . . once they get done, there's like a little machine in your head and it puts it onto a conveyor belt and drops it down to your throat and then down to your tummy. *(We both laugh.)*

Like many adults, Jolene is fascinated with how her mind works—how she can remember and record information—and where that information gets stored in her body for later retrieval. Later in the same day, during writing workshop, she further developed her idea into a kind of blueprint for memory—her "memories box"—which she described to her friend Michelle (see Figure 6.1):

Excerpt from Fieldnotes, February 1, 1990

JOLENE: This is a memory box and here's the brain person, and they have all your different memories in little boxes wrapped up, and then when you use them, you unwrap them . . . and then . . .

MICHELLE: Wait a sec! They wrap up all your memories?

JOLENE: And then they put names on them.

RUTH: Oh, they label them? They put a name on it?

JOLENE: They know what they are, and then they take them to the conveyor belt and it comes down to here, and then these little robots put it on this rope,

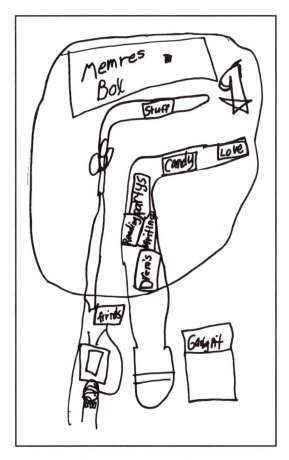

Figure 6.1   Jolene's "memories box"

when there's enough room, and then it will go back up, and then this brain person . . .

(Isabelle looks up from her own drawing and listens intently to the conversation, then looks at the picture.)

ISABELLE *(pointing to the star-shaped body to the right of the "stuff" label in Jolene's picture):*   What's this?

JOLENE: That's the brain person.

RUTH: That's the brain person . . . What does it say here?

JOLENE: "Stuff." This is all the stuff, and this is "reading," "writing," "dreaming," "candy," "love," "friends" . . .

RUTH: And so these are all the things you have to store . . .

JOLENE: Mmm-hmm. It's *(giggles)*—I don't know why! I just, I was just thinking!

RUTH: Well, we were talking about how you have all this stuff that you remember in your head, and where do you keep it all!

JOLENE: I need to draw the thing—down here, it's called the garbage pit, and then when they find stuff they don't need any more, 'cause they don't need to remember it, they just toss it in there.

RUTH: Oh, so there's some things that your brain doesn't really need to remember . . .

JOLENE: Uh-uh, any more.

RUTH: It gets chucked in the garbage? What are some examples of kinds of things you don't need to remember?

JOLENE: Like, your library book, 'cause once you take it to the library, you don't need to remember that any more. In P.E. we don't need to remember how fast we ran. We don't need to remember that any more.

(Don joins us.)

MICHELLE *(to Don):*   Did you see what Jolene drew? She drew a—wanna explain it?

With further explanations, Jolene continued to refine her theory of how memories work. Her discussion sparked for me how important it is to explore the invisible workshop that goes on inside children's minds—and the key role of memory within that workshop. Clearly, memory is a key component in learning, but it is even more than that. Memory lays the foundation for creative options. In classrooms that nurture creativity, children's memory structures must be developed and stimulated.

The last twenty years have seen a dramatic growth in our understanding of memory—and a move beyond its being seen as a passive recording of information. In creating these new theories, researchers have focused on many of the same elements that Jolene detailed in her "memories box." If we want to reorganize classroom learning situations to help children develop the kinds of memory processes that will nurture their creative development, we need to understand three of the aspects of memory that concern Jolene and the researchers: how memories are acquired, how they are stored, and how they are retrieved. Rather than the computer model that so many theorists in the past have relied on, contemporary memory theory likens the brain to more of a "chemical soup." As Gretel Ehrlich eloquently writes, "We are elaborate biorhythmic, electrical, emotional organisms, with a mass of systems so intricate no computer could begin to track what happens to the body when a single thought registers there" (1994, p. 88).

ACQUIRING MEMORY

Memory creates a context for understanding what we detect. In a very real sense, it is memory that allows us to see and hear. Physicist Leon Cooper, and other leading researchers in the field of memory, believe that memory is a construct, not a simple rerunning of a mental videotape (Johnson 1991). The brain works as a whole community of neural networks, and memories are spread like smoke throughout the brain. George Johnson explains, through an example, how perception and memory merge into one:

> Looking out the window at the ocean, we might notice a bright light in the night sky hovering in the horizon. Deep inside the brain one neural network responds to this vector, dismissing it as just another star. But its intense brightness causes another network to guess that it is Venus. Then, the light starts getting bigger, brighter, creating a different vector, a different set of firing patterns. Another network associates this configuration with approaching headlights on a freeway. Then, two more lights appear, green and red. Networks that interpret these colors feed into other networks; the pattern for stop light weakly responds. All over the brain, networks are talking to networks, entertaining competing hypotheses. Then comes the roar, and suddenly we know what it is. The noise vector, the growing-white-light vector, the red-and-green-light vector all converge on the network—or network of networks—that says *airplane*. (1991, p. 165)

When different people are presented with the same event, their brains will pick up different features to put into their memory structures, and will continue to build on these features in different ways. Some people's brains might tell them they had seen a UFO or a heavenly visitor instead of an airplane; it depends on what is already stored in their brain. When the perceptions of several different brains overlap, we have some agreement about what constitutes reality. "In the brain and in society," Johnson concludes, "hordes of neural networks compete for the most plausible interpretation of the signals we receive from our world, matching them as best they can in a way that resonates with the past" (1991, p. 165).

Jolene has created "brain people," like neural networks, that decide how to name our experiences, whether reading or writing, parties or candy, friends or love. But the real "brain people"—neural networks—don't put our memories into the neat and tidy boxes that Jolene imagines; it's a much messier process. As neurophysiologist William Calvin explains, "Unlike computer memories that store things in pigeonholes, a memory such as 'elephant' is stored in a distributed way throughout whole areas of the brain, overlapping with other memories in ways we do not yet understand" (Calvin and Ojemann 1994, p. 47).

STORING MEMORY

For the past fifteen years, memory theorists have moved away from looking at memory in terms of duration (short- and long-term). As Barry Schwartz and Daniel Reisberg put it, "The labels 'short-term' and 'long-term' memory are misleading . . . Short-term memories don't have to be short; long-term memories don't have to be long. Moreover, these terms invite confusion over whether 'medium-term' memories form a distinct category, and so on. In short, using these labels simply draws our attention to a less than informative feature of memory" (Schwartz and Reisberg 1991, p. 281).

Instead, researchers are focusing on an alternative approach through what is called "levels of processing." (For a more detailed discussion of the drawbacks of short-term and long-term memory modality theory, and a thoughtful description of the levels-of-processing approach, see Schwartz and Reisberg 1991, Chapter 7.) This approach to memory can have an enormous impact on classrooms, teachers, and the ways that learning environments are structured. Our creativity depends on our access to our memories; the more sophisticated and deep our structures, the larger our capacity for the kinds of mental leaps that help us connect seemingly dissimilar thoughts into patterns, or create new metaphors.

Levels of Processing

Contemporary memory theorists from fields as diverse as biology (Gary Lynch), physics (Leon Cooper), philosophy (Patricia Churchland), neurophysiology (William Calvin), and psychology (John Anderson) are all studying the *processes* of how and where memories reside in the brain. They are moving beyond the image of memory as a passive, simple recording of information and exploring the ways that the brain takes the patterns it perceives and builds mental maps and theories of how the world works through memory processing.

The cornerstone of the processing theory is that we have some control over how we think about information in our environment—especially how deeply we choose to think about it. At a superficial level, we do what Craik and Lockhart (1972) call *shallow processing*. In Jolene's model, this is the "garbage pit" information, "like [when] your library book [is due]" or "how fast we ran in P.E." In terms of the printed word, it might be the surface features of something, such as the color of letters or whether they are upper- or lowercase.

It is *deep processing* that explores what words mean, what connotations are called up—and it is only deep processing that leads to strong memory formation (Craik and Lockhart 1972; Lockhart, Craik, and Jacoby 1976;

Anderson 1985). So, rather than focus on shallow features, like individual letters or whether they are upper- or lowercase, we need to look at the deeper meanings in order to help young children form memories that are meaningful and will contribute to the depth of their learning.

Strategies such as urging children to "memorize" spelling or math facts are unlikely to succeed. It is far more important for teachers to encourage children to think deeply about the material they are working with—and to provide ways for them to do so.

Creating Deeper Memory Processing in the Classroom

In a study of life cycles, Nancy Winterbourne gave her second-grade students the opportunity to process the information they were learning by writing and reflecting in their science journals. On the first page of her journal (Figure 6.2), Jolene wrote what she had learned from the film strip they had watched and the story Nancy had read to them:

> Caterpillars spin webs. The little balls are waste stuff. They eat leaf jello. A butterfly lays an egg as big as this: [picture of eggs]. They lay a bunch together. The metamorphosis is a miracle. A caterpillar makes a chrysalis or cocoon.

Nancy also provided firsthand experience with life cycle observations by setting up a "Butterfly Garden" in the classroom, where the children observed the butterfly metamorphosis, from caterpillar to mature Painted Lady butterfly, as they wrote and drew their observations daily in their journals (Hubbard 1993).

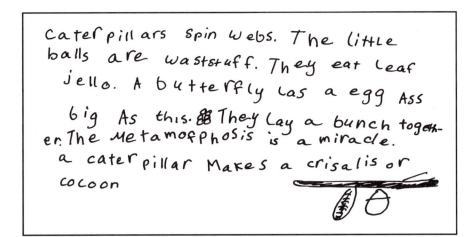

Figure 6.2 Jolene's science journal entry

Their continuing to observe the life cycle changes and write about the process as it occurred gave depth to their memory-forming processes. Cindy wrote and drew detailed observations as she noticed the daily changes (see Figure 6.3):

Thursday, May 3, 1990
I saw some holes in the leaf jello where the caterpillars had took a bite. One of the caterpillars likes to climb up the jar.

Friday, May 4, 1990
Today all the caterpillars were climbing up the jar. One caterpillar took a slow dive onto the leaf jello and took a bite after he was up a little.

Monday, May 7, 1990
The caterpillars are getting bigger. It looks really gross the way the leaf jello is splattered all over. The caterpillars I think have shed their skin twice. When I first saw the leaf jello, it made me want to throw up.

May 9, 1990
The caterpillars are all on the top hanging from the lid. I think they're making chrysalises. If they are, then pretty soon they'll be butterflies.

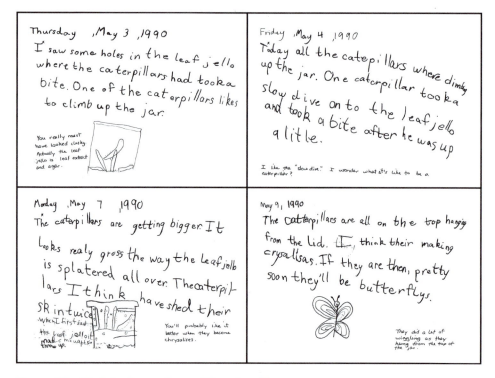

Figure 6.3   Cindy's observations of the caterpillars

Cindy is learning more deeply about the life changes as she constantly reflects on what she is observing, reading, writing about. She uses the terminology effortlessly in her journal, commenting on the chrysalis that is growing, and what this growth means as a stage of development in the butterfly's life. She is able to connect her knowledge to her own memory structure, making important creative leaps: she sees the "slow dives" that the caterpillars make, or invents a term like "leaf jello" for the agar that the caterpillars eat. Nancy's daily written responses to the children's science journals are important, too. She confirms their observations, reinforces correct terminology, and wonders along with the children as they make predictions.

Writing is a vital tool in helping memory formation; it helps us focus on meaning and the process of learning itself. Being aware of our processes and the learning strategies we call into use makes them more accessible the next time. In Jill Ostrow's class, the children expect to be asked to explain how they solved problems or explored concepts. These explanations are a part of the problem solving itself.

Look at Taylor's explanation of how she added 7 plus 5 (Figure 6.4). She uses drawing, letters, and numerals to help her solve this problem: "I used

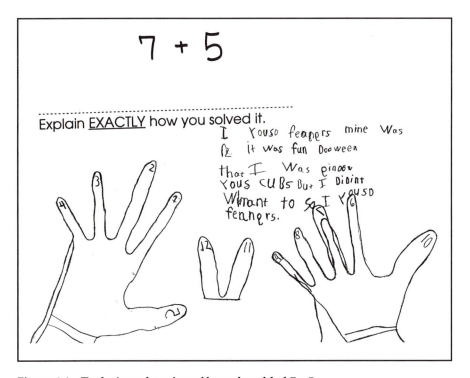

Figure 6.4   Taylor's explanation of how she added 7 + 5

fingers. Mine was 12. It was fun doing that. I was going to use cubes, but I didn't want to, so I used fingers."

Tara takes her 8 × 3 problem to a deeper level of processing with her written explanation as well (see Figure 6.5): "I know that the × in 8 × 3 means you times the number before it. The other number means how many times you times 8. So I drew 8 circles 3 times."

In a more sophisticated long-term project, the children in Jill's class designed a forest. Throughout this project, they wrote about their learning processes. The children paired up and began by solving a problem—to come up with an area that was not a square and was at least 225 square units. Spencer wrote about the tools and processes he and Joseph used as they wrestled with the dimensions:

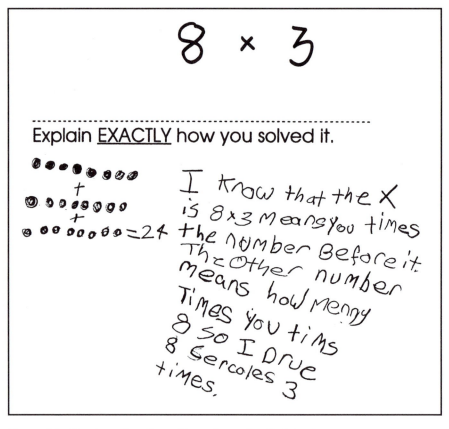

Figure 6.5   Tara's explanation of how she multiplied 8 × 3

I used unifix cubes. I am working with Joseph. I found out that 15 by 15 was 225. How I figured that out was, I went 15 × 15 was 225. Then me and Joseph made the square and Joseph put 15 unifix cubes next to a ruler and found out that it was almost a foot and started to take out and put in. First I took out 8 and put in 8 somewhere else and then Joseph took out three from the side and put it in somewhere else. The End.

While Spencer wrote a detailed description on his own, other children needed to be nudged to deeper processing. Seth's first attempt was short and sweet: "I made a square and put new parts in it." In a brief conference with him, Jill urged Seth to think back on all the resources he had used. He then added: "That is not all what I did. I used cubes. That is all what I did." When Jill read his next version, she realized she needed to be more directive, as well as give him a chance to talk through his process prior to writing. "Seth, that is *not* all that you did. Explain to me how you came up with 20 times 20."

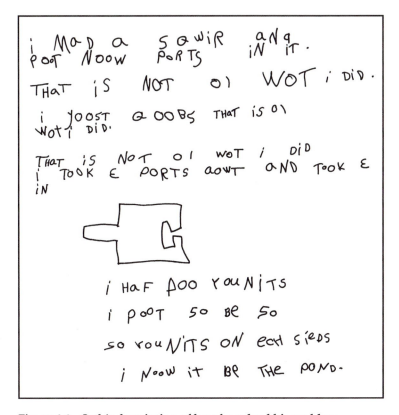

Figure 6.6   Seth's description of how he solved his problem

After their conversation, Seth was able to write his final addendum (Figure 6.6):

> That is not all what I did. I took 3 parts out and took 3 in. I have 400 units. I put 20 by 20. 20 units on each side. I knew it by the pond.

Seth's final sentence is extremely important: "I knew it by the pond." The "pond" was actually a previous design problem that the children had worked on, one that was less complex, but that also required them to work with square units. Rather than working on disconnected pieces of learning, Seth and the other children are urged to build on their knowledge and to be aware that this is an important strategy for continued learning. Seth knows that he learned from the pond design tools that he can use to help solve the design problems he will encounter as he works on this new forest design challenge. He is developing strategies for future innovative thinking.

The more connections and different strategies for processing information we can use, the deeper our memory formations and the more wide-ranging our neural networks will be. With more specific thinking about different nuances of meaning and multiple interpretations, another principle of processing, *elaborate processing*, comes into play. "Thinking about an event's meaning (deep processing) does lead to better memory than thinking about an event's superficial appearances (shallow processing)," Barry Schwartz and Daniel Reisberg explain, "but thinking about multiple aspects of an event's meaning (elaborate processing) helps even more" (1991, p. 283). In other words, finding many connections between what you know and what you learn and exploring multiple perspectives are immensely important.

Some children make these connections spontaneously. When Nancy Winterbourne and I were exploring children's strategies as they learned to read, we noticed that the more proficient readers in her second-grade class connected their personal experiences to stories that they heard and read in their journals. Annie's delightful response to *A River Dream* (Say 1988) is a particularly telling example (see Figure 6.7). The first page reads, "I like the story you read. It made me think of all the fishing trips I've went on. I like it." On the next page, Annie drew a tiny teacher sitting in a rocking chair and reading, dwarfed by Annie and her huge mental image of herself with her friend fishing. The final page of her journal entry features Annie herself in the middle of the page behind a paper door that opens and closes with her appreciative response to the "very nice story."

Nancy and I saw more and more such evidence, which demonstrated how important it is for children to use their background knowledge as an aid to understanding what they read. We hoped to find ways to activate their memories in connection to their reading, bring this information out to be examined

Figure 6.7   Annie's three-page response to *A River Dream*

and shared, and help create that more elaborate memory processing that will aid children's literacy development. And beyond improvement of their reading ability itself, we wanted to find ways they could make more creative links to their reading, based on their own individual ways of making sense of the world. We created a format for reading response journals that would help children who weren't making these connections spontaneously.

Nancy was reading *Charlie and the Chocolate Factory* (Dahl 1977) to the children at the time, so we began by asking the children to respond in their reading journals to two different aspects of the book: their favorite part and what it reminded them of. Jeannie and Cindy linked the book to their different experiences. Reading about a character going up in the glass elevator brought to Jeannie's mind the physical experience of going up and down quickly: "It reminds me of when I jumped on a trampoline—Wheeee!" Cindy, on the other hand, is reminded of candy bars—and not wanting to share them: "It reminds me of when I buy a candy bar with my allowance and my sister wants it." The visual depiction of her sister's screaming face, nose in the air, bellowing "I want a candy bar!" is countered by Cindy herself in the corner, calmly "crunch crunch"-ing, with the words "Forget it" in the word bubble over her head.

Aisha, a rather literal reader, found our request a daunting task. When I conferred with her as she sat at her desk chewing on her pencil, she repeated what she had written: "Well, I don't know." Her final paper shows a picture of the classroom, with Nancy asking her, "What does it remind you of, Aisha?" and Aisha's response: "I don't know!"

The children brought these pages to their discussions of the story and heard each other's stories, which often sparked new connections. Aisha commented in the discussion that it made her "sort of wish she had a real chocolate factory," a leap for her, in that she had made a personal connection to her reading. Because of this and other discussions, Nancy continued to ask the children to make written connections to the books they chose to read during reading workshop. Though they were all reading different books of their choice, they would bring their responses to their small-group discussion and "book talks," sharing their personal stories and their reading adventures. Focusing their reading discussions in this way occasionally (about once a month) seemed to help the children make deeper connections. Aisha soon learned to bring her background knowledge to her reading, and so forged new links to comprehension, as did Garth, who responded to a book he read with an experience he shared with his cousin (Figure 6.8). Other children found links to past reading experiences; Celeste wrote and drew about similarities and differences between the princesses in *Saint George and the Dragon* (Hodges 1984) and *The Paper Bag Princess* (Munsch 1980).

Your Name _Garth_

Title of the Book _Arthur's Techer Trowble_

Today's Date _____

Draw a picture of your favorite part of the book.

Write one or two sentences explaining your drawing.

"when Binky burns, says
The kids "make one   wrog move" and he
sa. puts you   on deathrow."
Mr. Ratbun
well do this

Draw a picture of what happens in your thoughts when you think

about this book. What does it remind you of?

Write one or two sentences to explain your ideas.

it rimeds me when me and my cosin
Ti bollons On are legs
and dress in stips

Figure 6.8   Garth's response to *Arthur's Teacher Trouble*

Elaborate processing of memories, writing about them and sharing multiple levels with others, helps bring people to deeper levels of understanding. The more widely knowledge is interwoven in one's memory structure, the more creative possibilities for future connections are available. Simply put, the more you know, the more you can connect to future learning.

Building a Community of Memories

Large-group discussions are another wonderful forum for elaborate memory processing. From individual connections, children can build a larger pool, with access to one another's memories as well. Jill's students close their reading workshop with a time when they talk about the books they are reading. She strives to create opportunities for them to make connections—and discuss them. In January 1995, when the children returned from their winter break, Jill asked them to choose a part of the book they were reading and tell the class what it reminded them of. Many of the main characters in the books they had chosen came alive for them because of the similarities to other children in the classroom: *Harold and the Purple Crayon* (Johnson 1955) reminded Ron of Micah, with his interest and ability in drawing; Matilda, the title character of Roald Dahl's book (1988), made Tara think of Jenna "'cause she knows so much and figures things out." Other children made connections to their lives outside of school, such as Jenna, who compared Brother Luke in *The Door in the Wall* (DeAngeli 1949) to the priest at her church, and Shauna, who delighted in the snow-filled pages of *Little Bear* (Minarik 1957) because it called to mind the rare winter storm that "blanketed" Portland, Oregon, with one inch of snow! Griffith was also reading *Little Bear* but instead of snow, he was reminded of "all our birthdays—even yours, Jill!"

The children's opportunities for deeper processing were heightened by the stories some children shared that sparked memories in the audience, generating new rounds of stories. Jeremy's humorous recounting of *Return to Howliday Inn* (Howe 1992) and how the animals reminded him of his pets created a ripple effect, with Travis adding anecdotes of how his sister's rabbit was like *Bunnicula* (Howe and Howe 1979). Julia started a new round of connections among literary figures when she talked about how reading *Baba Yaga* (Kimmel 1991) reminded her of witches in other stories. Kelly added a surprising connection when she talked about how the picture book *Are You My Mother?* (Eastman 1960) reminded her of the main character in the series of books Jill had read to them about Addie, a young girl from Civil War times (Porter 1993). "It reminded me of Addie 'cause she's always looking for things, too, and finding people in her family."

RETRIEVING MEMORY

 Where in the brain do these memories reside, and how can we get them activated? In Jolene's memories box, the brain people find the pieces they have labeled and bring them up as needed. Older theories of memory favored that kind of computer model; but, as already noted, it's a far messier system than this. William Calvin stresses that the most important thing to remember about human memory is to "think *process* rather than *place*" (Calvin and Ojemann 1994, p. 123). His memory metaphor is not of a computer, but a message board in a stadium, "with lots of little lights flashing on and off, but creating a pattern. In time and space" (p. 129).

How do we gain access to those patterns? It goes back to how memories are acquired and saved. Good retention results from deep, elaborate processing. Schwartz and Reisberg contend that these forms of processing aid memory "by laying down *retrieval paths* from the context to the to-be-remembered items themselves" (p. 408). The context is key. The deeper the processing, the more distinctive and varied the codes the brain creates; the more associations the brain creates, the more neural networks are activated.

In helping children acquire, store, and retrieve memories, the context for learning becomes all-important. What we learn in a rich context, with the variables that make it a "real-world" situation, we are far better able to use in the future. Creative thinkers need to be able to call up memories and apply them in novel ways across a range of situations. In contrast, for example, simply memorizing a list of vocabulary words makes for shallow processing. On Calvin's message board, few bulbs will light up, and there will be little access to them through neural networks. Words and concepts learned through whole stories, classroom episodes and explorations that make connections to prior learning, however, will light up the whole board with complex paths and neural highways, allowing new connections to be sparked.

In the past, teachers relied on tests and examinations to assess how well children retrieve memories and information. Even today, this ritual brings closure to certain units of study in the classroom. But what we now know about how the brain builds neural networks to retrieve memory explains why this strategy of "teach, then test, then go on to the next chunk to teach and test" works against children's continued learning and their ability to build on their knowledge and stretch it in new and exciting ways. Learning something for a test encourages shallow processing, which doesn't become incorporated into the complex mental architecture that we hope to build for children. They will have far more ability to retrieve their memories when they are immersed in learning as a by-product of their interest and investment in the learning process itself.

Children who are part of a community whose members think deeply about their experiences in learning can be encouraged to remember where they have been together as a class. We can build new rituals, where children generate stories and reminiscences of what they've learned together and how it connects to their new learning endeavors. Rather than seeing the closure of a long-term project as an ending, they can see it as opening new doors, spiraling outward to wider and wider experiences, which in turn they will build on and take in surprising new directions.

WHAT ELSE CAN WE DO IN THE CLASSROOM?

It's a mushy kind of information processing that goes on inside the head, no good at all for calculating pi to seventeen decimal places or for instantly retrieving telephone numbers. But for other kinds of tasks—recognizing a face that has aged ten years since the last encounter, reading graffiti, understanding words pronounced in many different accents, songs sung in any key—the mushiness is an advantage.

GEORGE JOHNSON

 Theories of how memory works—the whats and wheres of how our brains form new neural networks and work together to build new patterns and concepts—are at an exciting stage. We are learning how important the messiness and mushiness of the learning process are. Our brains have a great degree of plasticity; they physically change every day as we are exposed to different situations and incorporate new memories into the structures that exist in our heads. In this chapter, I have explored only a few of the basic ideas that current researchers are studying; I believe these ideas should have an impact on how we structure creative learning situations for children.

Deep processing is vital to good memory formation and access to memories. The more that children—and adults—can experience, write about, reflect on, talk about, and share multiple perspectives, the richer their learning will be and the more they will be able to make leaps in their thinking and continue to form new mental patterns and concepts. *Genuine, context-rich situations for learning* help us store memories more widely, giving us access to them across a range of future learning endeavors.

A third learning concept is an important connecting thread in the examples in this chapter: the importance of *building on prior knowledge*. Stephen Spender emphasized the importance of remembering and building on experiences to poets; Paul Gauguin relied on visual recall in his paintings (John-Steiner 1985). Other creative thinkers, such as mathematician Stan Ulam, cite the importance of memories of experience in enabling us to build analogies and so develop new ideas:

It seems to me that good memory—at least for mathematicians and physicists—forms a large part of their talent. And what we call talent or perhaps genius itself depends to a large extent on the ability to use one's memory properly to find analogies, past, present, and future, which are essential to the development of new ideas. (1976, p. 181)

Young children, too, need to be encouraged to mentally record their experiences and to create personal inventories of what they know and remember. This can help them make connections between their present knowledge and new ideas and insights.

How can we help children build on the memories they have? The most fundamental way is to encourage their worlds, stories, and experiences by allowing them to have a central role in the classroom. Rather than assigning topics to write about and books to read, teachers should encourage students to build personal inventories through portfolios, topic lists, and the centrality of individual choice in the classroom.

In writing, for example, we could never assign the kinds of topics that children choose to write when they draw from their own experiences. Six-year-olds Ming and Tinita talked with me about how they think up the topics they write about:

"I think about it at home," Ming explained. "Sometimes before breakfast. And lots of times when I'm walking to school, I'm thinking about it, thinking about it. But then," she added, "when I'm on Wednesday Hill, it's too steep. I can't think of topics then."

Tinita looked up from her writing long enough to comment, "I think about it when I'm eating dinner, then try to remember in the morning. Sometimes it's hard to remember and I have to think back in my mind."

"Yeah, like this morning," Ming agreed. "At breakfast, bones went through my mind, so I'm writing about the cow bones I found in my yard."

Every morning Ming, Tinita, and the other children in their first grade enter the classroom, take out their writing folders, reach into their bag of memories, and write. Like adult authors, they think about their writing when they're not writing, "thinking back in their minds" to remember, so they can create their stories. The best way to help students create the personal inventories that are essential to their creative growth is to make student choice a cornerstone of the curriculum.

Teachers who work with students of all ages have documented the integral role of choice in the growth of students' ability to acquire expertise and self-motivated learning, building from their memories and knowledge bases (Rief 1992; Ohanian 1992; Romano 1987; Hansen 1987; Graves 1994; Murray 1982). And from a workshop environment that offers them time to learn, children can make choices about what they need to support their growing strengths as learners. "Isn't that what education is all about?" asks Susan Ohanian (1992). "Helping people make their own choices? Helping them establish some sort of criteria for making good choices? Who's going to provide the core books for our students when they're on their own?" (p. 77).

Beyond making choices in topics to write about and books to read, students need to make choices among a range of modes of expression. They need to experiment with a variety of strategies to solve problems, investigate the questions that intrigue them, and make connections between new information and old. Self-knowledge and the encouragement to build on what they know are key elements for students; these elements help students acquire the practice they need to start their own creative processes.

In interviews with children who are in the midst of creative endeavors, as well as reflections by adult creative thinkers, the role of memory comes up again and again. And not surprisingly, it is *memory images* that individuals describe vividly as part of their creative process. All mental images are not memory images, of course, but mental imagery is composed largely of combinations and recombinations of images in our memory. Memory images form the cornerstone of children's mental imagery system, the subject of the next chapter.

RESOURCES

The following books are the ones I have found most useful for exploring the architecture of memory within our brain, and I encourage interested readers to dig into them. In addition to the topics discussed in this chapter, there are other exciting avenues of memory theory to explore, such as the idea of a Narrator in the mind, the importance of episodic memory as opposed to working memory, how implicit and explicit memory use different amounts of energy—just some of the fascinating ideas that can be investigated through these volumes.

Conversations with Neil's Brain: The Neural Nature of Thought and Language by William H. Calvin and George A. Ojemann (Reading, MA: Addison-Wesley Publishing Co., 1994). In the context of a kind of surgical drama, readers are witnesses to the mapping of a patient's brain in the midst of his surgery. Asides by the surgeon and the author supplement conversations with Neil's brain, bringing to life how language, memory, and decision making operate within the brain.

In the Palaces of Memory: How We Build the Worlds Inside Our Heads by George Johnson (New York: Alfred A. Knopf, 1991). Biologists, physicists, psychologists, and philosophers join in a search to discover the secrets of memory. Johnson weaves together the new tools and theories that these different disciplines are forging in coming to a new understanding of the brain and the mind.

Learning and Memory by Barry Schwartz and Daniel Reisberg (New York: W.W. Norton and Co., 1991). In presenting recent research in memory and learning, the authors explain how memory structures are integral to our learning processes. A notable strength of the book is its coverage of the psychology of the human memory, from information acquisition and storage to its retrieval and loss.

7

Mental Images in Children's Creative Processes

Putting away groceries, thinking ahead to making supper, I reached for the radio knob and flicked on the local news to hear: ". . . fire at a Wilsonville apartment complex. Three children are believed to be trapped in the fire . . ." Instantly, all my thoughts were directed to the children in Jill's class. Images of the apartment complex I had seen so often; of Maria and Esperanza, who wrote and talked about the apartments they lived in, flashed into my mind—with horrifying new images: of the building engulfed in flames and smoke, of the children frightened, hurt. I spent the rest of evening making frantic phone calls and switching channels to get all the local news coverage. By morning, I knew that though none of the children in Jill's class had been injured, several families were now homeless, and one child from the school had perished in the flames. I found myself reliving the moment of hearing the news flash, the initial shock of the news, and the images from the television as well as the ones I created in my mind.

Events happen suddenly in our lives. All of us affiliated with the school were affected by this tragedy that struck without warning. The images that haunted me that evening filled all our minds and are now etched into our memories. In fact, whether we want to or not, we will most likely recall these events more vividly than many other events that occurred that week because of the emotional content.

In all our histories, we have moments that stand out in sharp relief in our minds. Some are national, public events such as the assassination of Martin

Luther King, Jr., the explosion of the *Challenger*, the celebration of the end of the Berlin Wall. Others are of a more personal nature: a special birthday celebration, getting a driver's license, graduation ceremonies—a devastating fire. The most clearly remembered events, whether pleasant or unpleasant, are those that are the most emotional (Schwartz and Reisberg 1991). Some of these memories are so intense that they call forth a range of vivid images and have been dubbed "flashbulb memories":

> To understand the label, think what it is like to sit in a darkened room and have a picture taken by flashbulb. The scenes just prior to and just after the flash are difficult to make out. The moment of the flash, however, stands out in stark clarity. You often feel, minutes after the flash, that you can still "see the scenes in your mind's eye" in full detail. Flashbulb memories are rather like that. (Schwartz and Reisberg 1991, p. 518)

Many of the children in Jill's class reported stark mental images that they needed to "get out of their heads" and onto paper. The fire was especially devastating for six-year-old Esperanza, who was once a resident of the apartments. During writing workshop, she poured her mental images into her writing and drawing. In her conversation with me, her voice reflected her sadness, and her picture vividly recalled the sensations she experienced at the scene of the fire (see insert page 3).

Excerpt from Fieldnotes, January 18, 1995

RUTH: So this is the building you live in? Or used to live in?

ESPERANZA: I lived in it for a long, long time.

TARA: It's the same apartment building, but she lived way far away from where the fire was.

ESPERANZA: I went over there . . . and this is the 'flection on my face.

RUTH *(misunderstanding):*   That's the expression on your face?

ESPERANZA: That's the *reflection.*

RUTH: Oh, the reflection of the fire? on your face? Oh, my gosh, 'cause you were really close to it?

ESPERANZA: And I seen the smoke, but I didn't know it was in our apartment. I was scared . . . and I'm really sad at the kids. It said on the news and I watched it, and I seen the fire in our apartments, but my mom and dad ran and then they went home and got us and then we went to see it and then the next day it was real bad. It, the back porch is blown off, and I feeled terrible. But the other 'partments were safe. The people were on time to get the fire away from the other houses, but *(pause)* it was bad. *(Pauses, then looks back at her paper, points at the letters, and reads:)* "Fire reflection on my face." And that's . . . I had a bow in my hair.

Esperanza's drawing of her face fills the page, the fire, smoke, and soot "reflecting" off of it. She includes the detail of the bow in her hair and the tears on her cheeks. Her brief text, represented by the two letters *F* and *R*, captures poetically the "flashbulb" mental image in her mind of the night of the fire.

Eight-year-old Tara sat at the same table with Esperanza and me, talking with us as we wrote and drew, and reading us her finished piece (see Figure 7.1):

Excerpt from Fieldnotes, January 18, 1995

TARA (*reading from her paper*):   "Last night, me and my mom were coming home from gymnastics. My mom saw a fire and thought it was the orchard, but I had a closer look and saw it was the apartments, so we went up the hill and this is what we saw." And then I drew a picture.

RUTH: Can you describe that to me?

TARA: It's a black road with two trees coming up . . . and then I drew the fire coming up and then I drew all the smoke.

RUTH: So, it really just—you couldn't even see the apartment building with all the fire and stuff . . .

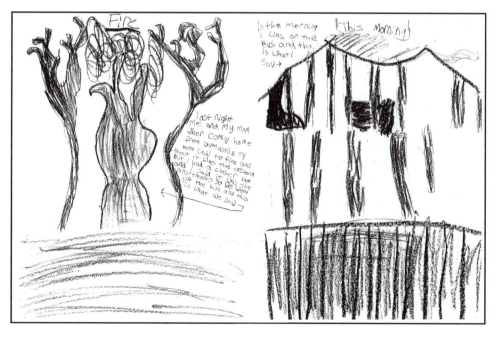

Figure 7.1   Tara's impressions of the fire. Left: Her mental image of the fire. Right: The next morning.

TARA: 'Cause of all the flames . . . Well, that's what I did, and then on the other side, I wrote, "In the morning I was on the bus and this is what I saw." And then I drew this building that's all black and that's all . . .

RUTH: Boy, it looked totally different in the morning. By that time, huh? Your drawings really show it . . .

TARA: It helped—it got it out of my mind, for one thing, and . . . *(Tara's voice trails off.)*

Not all the images the children report seeing in their mind's eye are as emotion-laden as those of the fire, of course. But as I have observed and interviewed children like Esperanza and Tara in the midst of their creative endeavors, it has become clear that images are a vital aspect of children's mental processes. The Latin word *imago*, meaning "image," is the root word of *imagination*. "The imagination is the image-forming faculty in the mind, the organ that has the power to clothe the beings of the inner world in imagery so that we can see them" (R. Johnson 1986, p. 22). Images are partners with words for making meaning; or as Will, one of the students in Nancy Winterbourne's second-grade classroom, told me one day, "The words and pictures—they're buddies."

Jenna demonstrated this for me graphically. When I asked her to explain what goes on in her mind while she is writing a story, she led me to a round table in the corner of the room, picking up a blank piece of paper on her way, explaining, "I'll draw my mind while I'm thinking of a story." She began by drawing a profile of a head with a few features attached (Figure 7.2), and as she worked, she commented on what she was doing:

Excerpt from Fieldnotes, October 6, 1993

JENNA: That's the eye, the nose . . . I'm just gonna draw a big, empty space for my mind . . . I'll just draw . . . see, I have words that are in my head. I talk to myself way more in my head than I do out loud. I tell myself "Once upon a time." *(She writes these words.)* and then I see a picture and it starts forming more and more . . .

RUTH: So is this picture in color? Or black and white?

JENNA *(pauses; thinks):* It's hard to describe. It's not really in color. This is a nymph guy that I'm drawing.

RUTH: So this picture sort of forms in your head while you're thinking of a story?

JENNA *(nods):* Then I keep thinking of it and it gets bigger. *(Points to the nymph.)* This is like something I form after "Once upon a time." And I hear him laughing in my head.

RUTH: So then you hear different voices than your own?

Figure 7.2 What goes on in Jenna's mind as she writes

JENNA: Yeah, I hear this guy's voice . . . When I see the pictures, sometimes I hear things. There are people moving around inside my head, but I don't see them with my eyes, I see them with my mind.

RUTH: So, you start writing, and then . . .?

JENNA: I write, then some of it stops in my head. Then, when I stop writing to think again, it starts moving again.

MEMORY IMAGES

Memory images are one important aspect of the complex architecture that creates our memory systems, and they are the building blocks for a range of other mental images. A memory image may be defined as "a reconstruction or resurrection of a past perception" (Horowitz

1970, p. 22). You can experiment with this right now. Picture in your mind's eye your childhood bedroom. Take a few moments. Can you "see" the door, windows, objects in your room? Most people imagine they are *in* the room, seeing what they would see from a perspective within that space. Not surprisingly, children describe this kind of memory image again and again as I talk with them about their creative processes.

Memory images appear to have a range of vividness: some children describe the images as bright and clear, others as vague and hazy. In keeping with research on flashbulb memories, the memories with the strongest emotion are usually the most vivid. Another aspect of these images that I found through interviews with children is that they are controllable: they can be summoned at will, and they can also be stopped if a person desires to move on to something else.

In composing meaning through reading, memory images are especially important. Kris, for example, told me that whenever he hears a story with a baby in it, the picture that comes to his mind is his own baby brother. When Steven shared Judy Blume's *The Pain and the Great One* (1974) with the class, Kris thought of his little brother, as his journal entry for February 5, 1990, shows: "That story that Steven read reminds me of my little brother. He digs in my mom's purse." The numerous examples in the previous chapter, from Annie's response to *A River Dream* (Say 1988) to Garth's remembrance of playing with his cousin, show the memory images that children call up—and their importance in building children's reading comprehension.

Children often rely on memory images as they think mathematically, too. Tara told me that when she solves "easy" problems, she often pictures her fingers in her mind and simply counts them. "Is it always fingers that you see, or do you ever see other kinds of things?" I wondered.

"Well, like tally marks. Each time there's, like, 5, I put a whole tally mark there in my head, and then if there's not, like 5 plus 5 is 10, but if it doesn't go to 10, then I just add marks, and then I count it up."

Ron also relied on counting the images he created in his mind's eye. Just after he finished solving a math problem, I asked him to explain to me how he had done it.

"Well, I had 36 dogs and 6 people, and I had to make it so each person had an even amount of dogs, and so I took away 6 from 36 until I got the answer and it was 6."

"Can you explain what went on in your head while you were doing it?"

"Sometimes when I try to solve problems, it's like I have a dogsled and people," Ron explained. "I thought about the dogsled and people for this . . . And like on one of the battlefield problems when we were in the Civil War, I thought of some people on the battlefield. Um, if there are 6 people, how many arms would they have all together . . . I thought of 6 people, and I counted their arms and that was 12."

When children create, then, they appear to rely on their memory images much the way Mozart describes his music composing process: "When I proceed to write down my ideas, I take out of the bag of my memories what has previously been collected into it" (quoted in Vernon 1975, p. 56).

IMAGINATION IMAGES

 What about imagination images? Where do these "new images" spring from? In a sense, memory images are the building blocks of imagination images. Children—in fact, all of us—rely on these imagination images, which "contain elements of past perceptions, but arranged in a different way than they were originally perceived" (Samuels and Samuels 1975, p. 43). Toni Morrison eloquently describes how she rearranges her memory images and reconstructs them in her fiction writing. Memory, she says, "weighs heavily in what I write . . . These 'memories within' are the subsoil of my work. It's a kind of literary archeology: on the basis of some information and a little bit of guesswork you journey to a site to see what remains were left behind and to reconstruct the world that these remains imply" (1987, pp. 111–112).

Seven-year-old Connie's picture book (Figure 7.3) is a wonderful example of how children use their creativity—and their imagination images—as they write. The story begins with Connie's memory image of her father's pet spider (Figure 7.3A): "Here is my Dad's spider." On the next page (Figure 7.3B), she again reached into her bag of memories to write about a real event: "Once he escaped." But as Connie drew, and added the fanciful picture of the door on that page, she began her flight of imagination, which triggered the rest of her picture book. The spider is lost, and looks around at images that surround him: a highway stretching across the horizon, and tall buildings. A word bubble coming out of his mouth says, "Hmm . . . This must be California" (Figure 7.3C).

I asked Connie how her spider knew that he was in California. Once again, images were important in her answer. She patiently explained to me that she's shown him lots of picture books, so he was able to recognize where he was!

Connie continued to recombine the different memory images that she held in her mind in order to create new imagination images, as her spider finds himself in various places (Paris), and even different times (encountering a woolly mammoth) (Figure 7.3 D, E, and F).

Figure 7.3   Connie's spider story

Imagination images are also vital in the introspection that is reported by physicists and mathematicians. Physicist George Gamow relied on imagery as an essential element of his scientific process:

Gamow possessed this ability to see analogies between models for physical theories to an almost uncanny degree. In our ever-more-complicated and perhaps oversophisticated uses of mathematics, it was wonderful to see how far he could go using intuitive pictures and analogies from historical or even artistic comparisons . . . His pioneering work in explaining the radioactive decay of atoms was followed by his theory of the explosive beginning of the universe, the "big bang" theory. (Ulam 1976, p. 183)

Albert Einstein also describes a "thought experiment" he conducted; after reading Maxwell's theorem, which proposed to explain light waves, "he imagined himself riding through space, so to speak, astride a light wave and looking back at the wave next to him" (John-Steiner 1985, p. 85).

Some children, like Einstein, also rely on their imagination images as they think mathematically. Jenna explained to me how she conjured up ten strips in her mind and mentally manipulated then, then went on to explain how she imagined herself writing out problems in her mind.

Excerpt from Fieldnotes, February 1, 1995

RUTH: OK, Jenna, if I ask you to add 18 and 12, what goes on in your head?

JENNA: Well, what's 8 plus 2, which is 10, so 10 plus 10 plus 10 is 30.

RUTH: What was going on in your head as you do that?

JENNA: Sometimes I think of 10 strips.

RUTH: Ten strips?

JENNA: Like, I see the 10 strips, they're just sort of floating.

RUTH *(laughs):*   So, are 10 strips a pretty helpful way for you to figure out . . .?

JENNA: Yeah! Sometimes I can pretty well see things.

RUTH: Like what would you see?

JENNA: Like 10 strips, maybe sitting on the platform or sitting in front of me. I can do that! And, um, sometimes, if I concentrate really hard, I can imagine that I'm writing it down on a piece of paper, the number plus the number—8 plus 2, and then I put a zero—1, 1, 1 is 30. Sometimes I can do that!

RUTH: Oh! So, it's not like you picture it so much in your head as you actually have a picture of yourself writing it in your head. Is that right?

JENNA: Yeah. It's like I'm looking at it, and I like close my eyes and I see myself writing it down, and then I think, like that's a zero, and there's a 1 there, and 1 plus 1 plus 1 is 3, so . . .

RUTH: That's terrific!

A characteristic of imagination images, at least with the groups of youngsters I have observed and interviewed, is the intensity of the children's attention to these images. Other thoughts seldom intruded or distracted them from their imagination images, which were overwhelmingly reported as clear and vividly colored. Like their memory images, though, the children did have control over them; they could be stopped when the students chose.

Second graders Garth and Tracey relied on recombining memory images in their responses to reading books. Garth's images of the land "where the wild things are" are a combination of the mental pictures he creates from reading the book itself and a projection of himself into that imagined land (Figure 7.4). In a similar way, Tracey imagines herself riding on Clifford, the big red dog, alongside Clifford's owner, Emily Elizabeth (Figure 7.5).

We seem to have a little less control with imagination images than with memory images; we are able to stop imagination images, but are in a more distracted state. Michelle described this well when she explained to me her

Figure 7.4   Garth in the land "where the wild things are"

Figure 7.5   Tracey riding Clifford, the big red dog

process in terms of *Charlotte's Web* (White 1952), which she chose to read to herself after her teacher, Nancy Winterbourne, had read it aloud to the class. "When Ms. Winterbourne reads it, you can sort of think it up in your head," Michelle told me. "I can't really explain how you see it in your head, but you do. Like right here, in the chapter "Before Breakfast," when I was imagining Henry being a clown. I was imagining him having blue overalls and a white shirt. That's the picture in my head." She paused and thought a minute. "It's like you're daydreaming with your eyes open. In color and everything."

DAYDREAM IMAGES

 When the notion of daydreaming appeared in children's conversations, as it did in Michelle's, I tried to follow up on it and learn how the children defined their daydream images—and how these images related to their creative work in the classroom. In the earlier conversation, for example, I probed further, asking Michelle, "Daydreams? What are your daydreams like?"

"Well," she considered. "I don't really have a lot. The only time I have daydreams is when I'm writing."

"Oh, and so what are they like?" I asked.

She pointed to the drawing before her. "Like in this one, I picture me in a boat catching a fish . . . I pictured me doing that." She struggled to explain her process. "I could picture me and I could draw the picture better."

"It sounds like you have a lot of pictures in your mind," I pointed out.

Michelle nodded. "Well, see, I try to think up as much as I can so I can share with some people and I try to think most of them up before I share."

We continued our discussion, with Michelle emphasizing how much daydreaming helps her writing, concluding, "[It helps] with *my* writing, anyway. With some people, I guess it can't, but with me, it really helps."

Michelle is not unique. Many children have talked with me about their tendency to daydream in the process of writing. Seven-year-old Danny told me he daydreams a lot. "But you know what?" he confided. "I daydream, but it's nothing new. It happened in the past and I think about it over and over again, and last summer I went to Water Ways. Have you ever went there?"

When I confessed that I hadn't, he proceeded to tell me all about the water slides and underground waterways, and it was several minutes before I could bring him back to his earlier contention that he always daydreams about episodes in the past, reliving them.

"So Danny, when you're daydreaming, you always dream about fun things that you've done before, but you don't dream up new things?"

He considered, then answered, "Mmm. Well, sometimes I do. Sometimes I think about when I, um—next Friday night, I'll go someplace and I'll daydream about what I'm gonna do. And stuff like that. If I get lost, what I would do."

This apparent contradiction points out the defining features of daydreaming images. They seem to be a combination of memory and imagination images. The children, like Danny, pictured people and scenes in ongoing situations. The people and places may or may not be known, and the situation may be past or future oriented. Children report reliving past events as they happened, as Danny did, or as they wished they had happened, as well as what they might do if a certain situation arises in the future.

How many times have you found yourself reliving a past situation? It might be as delightful as slowing down time and remembering each moment of a delicious romantic encounter, or as painful as recreating an embarrassing teaching moment, then daydreaming about what you might have said or done that would change the situation dramatically.

What daydreams introduce into mental imagery that is different—and very important in narrative writing, in storyline recognition, and in mental development—is a time factor. "In general, daydreams deal with a series of images, more or less in chronological order, in which events take place" (Samuels and Samuels 1975, p. 46). Angie's prewinter break daydreaming is a good example of that key time element. She wrote, "For Christmas, we are going to go to the beach and then when we come home on Christmas morning, we are going to my other grandma's and grandpa's house and then we are going to go home and open our presents." With her writing, she attached a drawing, where she projected ahead into the future, showing the morning trip to the beach with the sun high in the sky; the evening at her grandma's with the sun and moon both in the sky, representing twilight; and then, finally, the return home, with the stars twinkling in the night sky.

Daydreaming, then, ties into a particular kind of memory images: memories of particular *episodes*, such as yesterday's dinner or last year's vacation. But daydreaming most often recombines our repertoire of memories so that they are also imagination images—projecting into the future possible episodes, or narrations of "when" and "what if." Daydreaming is intimately connected with our inner voice, or what is sometimes called our Narrator (Calvin and Ojemann 1994). Our Narrator is that voice that emerges in our brain and somehow pulls together the stories we have constructed about our past, in the process helping us see ourselves poised at a crossroads between our various stories about the past and our imagined futures.

Kathy's journal entry about her daydream of what school would be like is a good example of this kind of projection into the future. In her mind, she pictures herself getting ready for the first day of school, and explains her excitement to her "dumb brother" (see Figure 7.6).

Author Gloria Naylor describes the importance of daydreaming in her creative process:

> I am very much a daydreamer. When I was younger, I used to literally daydream serials . . . I was always the star. It was always me, five years later, or older, in some situation I thought pleasing . . . I'm still a very elaborate daydreamer. When I'm stuck in the writing of a book I will lay down and play it out in my mind to get myself past that bump some way . . . try to get a mind picture of what I want to happen. Then I'll get up and go back to the word processor and attempt to look for words for that mind picture. (quoted in Epel 1993, p. 168)

Kay was another child in Nancy Winterbourne's second-grade class who often referred to daydreams in relation to her process as a writer and a reader. She explained to me, "When I daydream, it's like it's night, only it's day."

"What happens in your mind when you daydream?" I asked.

Figure 7.6   Kathy's daydream about the first day of school

"Uh, well, see, it makes pictures like when I remember, only it's a *new* thing."

"So," I asked, "how are the pictures different when you're making up a new thing in your daydreams?"

"They kinda make sense with the words, like, see, when I read this . . ." and she read an excerpt from a book she had been practicing reading: "'Deep in the country there was—once—lived a merchant who had fallen on hard times.' When I read this, I make little conversations in my head to go with the pictures."

Compare Kay's comment about "making pictures like when I remember, only it's a *new* thing" to novelist Anne Rice's reflections on her process: "To me, daydreaming is intimately connected with writing. Writing is like day-dreaming. It's putting down in dramatic form whatever is on your mind. Daydreams are some sort of code for whatever concerns you. I can't really imagine what the minds are like of those who can't daydream or fantasize because I'm so used to doing it. So, my writing grew out of that, obviously" (quoted in Epel 1993, p. 210).

Daydreaming and fantasizing are important in reading as well as in writing. This was confirmed through numerous conversations I had with children as they read. Jenna, for example, had just finished reading *Otherwise Known as Sheila the Great* (Blume 1972). "What happened in your head while you were reading that?" I asked.

"I felt like I was Sheila. Like, I felt like I was scared of dogs—it was a 'me story.'"

Intrigued, I asked, "What's a 'me story'?"

"It sounds like it's happening to you because they say 'I' and 'me,'" Jenna explained. "That's the main character. Then I feel like I'm that person." She paused to draw another outline of her head (Figure 7.7), added Sheila within her "mental space," and continued to explain her process.

"It's kind of like with writing. When I start reading, the figures stop moving around. Then when I stop, I'm sort of daydreaming and they start moving around again."

In her picture, Jenna carefully drew multiple arms and legs to show the movement that was occurring within her daydreaming episodes, as she felt them happening to her.

Literary space refers to a psychological place—"a state of mind in which the reader blurs the distinction between reality and art" (Jacobsen 1982, p. 22). I found that the children I work with often inhabit and describe this literary space, a kind of daydream state that represents deep involvement with literature.

Jenna's description of "me stories" and her feeling as though she's that person as she reads struck me as just the kind of experience with literature that Norman Holland (1975) describes in adult readers: "People get involved . . . in three closely related ways: they cease to pay attention to what is outside the work of art; they concentrate their attention solely on it; then—and this is the special and important thing—they begin to lose track of the boundaries between themselves and the work of art . . . What is 'out there' in the literary work feels as though it is 'in here' in your head" (pp. 66–67).

This is just the kind of deep involvement with literature we want for children as well—and is clearly evidenced in my interviews with children as young as six. And the talk of children like Danny and Kay and Jenna of their involvement in daydreams points out another characteristic of this kind of inner image: the children showed more involvement and absorption in their

Figure 7.7   What goes on in Jenna's mind as she reads

daydreams than in either memory or imagination images. So although children are able to stop a daydream at will, it often takes more of an effort; they are more likely to forget themselves as they become engrossed in their inner world.

DREAM IMAGES

There is a state of mental imagery over which we have little or no control, of course: the dream state. Through the centuries, creative thinkers have often referred to their dreaming as vital in planning and in making breakthroughs that have eluded them in their more conscious states.

One morning in the spring of 1974, William Styron woke to the lingering image of a woman he had known in his early twenties. He could see her standing in a hallway, her arms full of books, the blue numbers of a tattoo visible beneath her sleeve. Suddenly he knew it was time to abandon the book over which he'd been laboring to tell this woman's story. He went directly to his studio and wrote the opening paragraphs of what was to become *Sophie's Choice*. (Epel 1993, p. 1)

In all of the classrooms I have spent time in, I see children writing about their dreams. Some write about dreams that have terrified them, like Will's "The Dead Mom," or Darrin's story about a nightmare (Figure 7.8): "I had a

Figure 7.8   Darrin's nightmare story

nightmare in my closet and I dreamed that he came out and squished my brain." Kathy's story took her several days to write, as she relived her frightening dream in her writing journal:

> I had a nightmare last night. You know those big whales that go in a swimming pool? Well, my sister has one and I slept on it last night and my nightmare is beginning. I was in the ocean and sharks were all around me and then I went under water and then a whale got me and brought me up and went back in . . .

Stephen King has the ability to tap into our deepest fears in his horror stories. He relates how childhood dreams are an important aspect of his creative process as well:

> I wanted to put [my character] in a spooky old house. I got about that far in my thinking and by whatever way it is that your mind connects things, as I was looking around for a spooky house, a guy who works in the creative department of my brain said, "Well, what about that nightmare you had when you were eight or nine years old? Will that work?" And I remembered the nightmare and I thought, "Yes, that's perfect." (quoted in Epel 1993, p. 136)

Much of children's writing about their dreams relates to happenings in the normal course of their lives rather than to bizarre and frightening situations. Angela wrote about her dream of what school would be like—typical of the kinds of dreams most of us experience when something new is about to happen in our lives. "Before the first day of school," she wrote, "I had a dream about the first day of school. I dreamed that I had a store in the school, and my room was hard to find, and our seats were hard."

Danny's piece about his dog is particularly interesting because he even gives his readers a picture of his inner dream images in relation to the reality of his bedroom (see Figure 7.9).

Children's dreams offer fertile ground for new ideas and creative insights. Like many adult authors, Connie found herself dreaming about the characters in her writing. As Connie was writing about a TV character named Vicki on the show *Small Wonder*, she dreamed about it. "I dreamed that I went to a rehearsal for *Small Wonder*." She continued to tell me about the dream and how that changed the direction of her writing, and then switched focus to the dream images themselves. She explained that the people in her dreams "looked like real people."

Some children told me about dreams they had had about what they were reading. Kay had had a very vivid dream about one of her favorite books, which she had been practicing reading, *Grandfather Twilight* (Berger 1984).

Figure 7.9   Danny's dream

"You had a dream about *Grandfather Twilight*? What happened?" I asked.

Kay ran to get the book from the library corner and pointed to a page. "It was here," she explained, "where he takes the pearl out of the trunk. And then I woke up right when he gave it to the sky."

"What did Grandfather Twilight look like in your dream?"

"He was different from the book. Instead of a white beard, he had brown. He looked kinda like my dad, the color of his eyes—my old dad."

Dreams often combine memory images and imagination images—familiar and unfamiliar images jumbled together. One big difference in dream images, though, is that the dreamer has little or no control over the images.

One morning, Darrin told me he had dreamed about Frog and Toad, characters from the book he had been reading (*Days with Frog and Toad*, Lobel 1979). In his dream, he was Frog, and his friend Eric was Toad. "We were having lots of fun, and walking around, going in the pool—and then the dream changed, and it was me and a rock star. And you know what? When I woke up, we were having a singing contest and in the dream, he won and got to spend the night at my house."

"You know," Darrin confided, "I can't see myself in my dreams. Except sometimes I can see my ears. It's more like I'm really in the dream."

Being "in the dream" has been reported by creative thinkers from writers to musicians to physicists. Stravinsky dreamed of the ritual that would be at the center of his ballet *Le sacre du printemps*. He saw himself there at the ritual and heard in his dream "the awakening of nature, the scratching, gnawing, wriggling of birds and beasts" that he later incorporated into musical themes (Stravinsky and Craft 1962, p. 159). Physicist John Howarth describes the way he "gets inside" his dream images: "I get inside them and wander about without any specific aim . . . looking at wires and cards, the elements of the images . . . This kind of thing often leads to productive insights" (John-Steiner 1985, p. 182).

MAKING ROOM FOR CHILDREN'S PROCESSES

 This range of mental images, from the vague recollections of the edges of childhood to vivid daydreams that project possibilities, helps creative thinkers approach ideas with visualization and intuition. Unfortunately, what is an accepted part of the process of creativity for adults is often ignored for young children, at least within most school settings. What can teachers do to help bring these elements into children's workshops of the possible?

One of the ways that Nancy Winterbourne creates spaces for children to wander in their minds and share visualizations is to create a daydreaming corner in the classroom, where the children can sit under a "dream-catcher," knowing they won't be disturbed as their thoughts take shape. She also guides them occasionally in creating images together. For example, one day, after reading the story *Frederick* (Lionni 1967) aloud to the children, she told them she was going to ask them to make a connection to the story of the little mouse who stored images in his mind.

Excerpt from Fieldnotes, September 12, 1989

NANCY: I'm going to say some words. See if you can have pictures. Let's see if we can do this with buses. Think back to a school bus trip that you've had.

Continuum of Mental Images

	Memory	Imagination	Daydream	Dream
			Continuum	
Imager's degree of control	High degree of control	Moderate degree of control	Some control	No control
Vividness and clarity	Ranges from clear and bright to hazy and vague	Very clear and vividly colored	Very clear and vividly colored	Varies
Composition of images	Reconstruction of past perceptions	Rearranged memory images	Series of imagination or memory images (in chronological order)	Memory and imagination images (jumbled together)

Ruth, you may have to think back a while. Just daydream in your mind how it was when you got on the bus. *(Pause.)* Does it smell differently? When you sit in a seat, do you have a special one, or do you choose it? *(Pause.)* What does your bus seat feel like? Just think about it. Is there someone you like to sit with? *(Pause.)* Pretend the bus is starting. What does the bus driver say? Where does the bus go? Picture in your mind. The bus gets close to your house. What does it look like outside the windows? What does it sound like inside the bus? What does it feel like when the bus driver opens the window? *(Pause.)* OK. How was that?

The children discussed what had happened in their minds, then Nancy concluded the discussion by saying, "I make a picture in my mind when I write. Maybe you do it differently, and that's fine. Wes, will you pass out the writing folders for writing workshop now?"

If the notion of visual thinking in the classroom is new to you, an easy place to start might be to encourage recollection of memory images, and creation of imagination images, connected to books that you read aloud to the class. For example, after I read *The Day of Ahmed's Secret* (Heide 1990) to Jill Ostrow's class, I asked them to close their eyes for a moment and tell what they see in their minds when they think about the story. In this picture book, Ahmed, a young boy in contemporary Cairo, shows readers a day in his city as he anticipates sharing a secret with his family in the evening. The children were quick to share their vivid images of the story. Daniel and Fiona started out by talking about the sights and sounds of the city and the ways it was similar to, and different from, our nearest city, Portland. "It has some cars, but not nearly as many as Portland, and tons more animals," Fiona noted. They also noticed that the streets in Cairo weren't as big as the ones in Portland, and that everyone in Cairo was walking.

Seth, on the other hand, found Cairo very much like Portland. "I see it like Portland—like downtown Portland, 'cause everyone's yelling and all those sounds."

Daniel chimed in, "And it has different things to do, there's Saturday Market . . . There's things to get."

Stephanie said she pretends she's in the pictures represented in the book: "I pretend like I'm the person from the different views; when you see the picture, it's like you're getting that view."

The discussion that grew from this image-finding exercise also gave me a lot of data about the children's understanding of and involvement with this story. The discussion quickly turned to family when Joseph said he pictured Ahmed sitting with his family. That sparked other kids to remember how hard it is to keep secrets in a family, as Ahmed did. Although they talked about their own secrets—such as Micah's not telling his mother about the coat they bought her, or Seth's reading his sister's diary—the discussion came back to Ahmed's secret when Maria said she remembered when she first learned to write her name. Her description of that memory image generated further discussion about memories of learning to write. Les told us, "When I first wrote my name, I wrote the L backwards at first."

Tara assured him that "lots of people write L's backwards at first." Then six-year-old Kelly told us, "When I was little, my sister said, 'If you want, I'll help you write your name.' I go, 'OK,' and she taught me how and we went to the library and got a library card."

The discussion veered far from the city of Cairo, yet the children were relating to Ahmed's story in that distant city. Perhaps most important, they showed their understanding of the story by the way they drew on their memories, often sharing the pictures they were seeing in their minds. They had a chance to experiment in a large group, imagining themselves within the pages of the book, seeing things from Ahmed's perspective. This experience can help them make similar connections when they read on their own.

Whole-class experiences with discussing mental images needn't be confined to reading stories; the discussions I had with children about how they solved math problems might easily evolve into children sharing and comparing their mental images as they think mathematically, or as they solve technology problems.

But in the long run, it's not so much creating new experiences as allowing what children need to do to flourish—to make room for their processes. Most of what I discovered from talking with the children simply happened as part of their workshop, because of the other conditions that were in place in the room. These children have choice in their writing and can use writing as a tool to work out important events in their lives. If they need to "get images out of their mind and onto paper," they have the freedom to do this, as Jill's class did after the fire in Wilsonville. If they have had dreams they want to write about, if they want to share the process of their vivid mental imagery in math problem solving, flexible workshop times allow them to do these things. In a sense, the most important strategy for teachers to adopt is to welcome into the classroom for children the same tools that we allow adult creative thinkers, and to give children the space to ponder their memories—to imagine, to daydream, and to dream.

8

Inner Designs: Children's Patterns of Thought

One morning as I surveyed the classroom, my eyes were drawn to eight-year-old Skip, who had put down his pencil, picked up a speckled turtle shell from his desk, and hummed softly as he turned it over in his hands. I approached his desk and sat down next to him.

Skip looked up at me. "I wanted to sort of draw down this song," he said. "I'll read it to you."

Songs

Sometimes I think up songs when I'm bored. my eastern mud turtle shell gave me an idea this morning. It goes like this. I have this little turtle his name is muddy mud, if you put him in some mud he'll swim and swim and swim and swim. singing eenee meenee minee moe. catch a turtle turtle by the toe if he hollers hollers let him go singing eenee meenee minee moe.

Skip began by reading his piece to me, but when he reached his song, he sang it to me, in a soft, clear voice.

The entire class was able to enjoy Skip's new composition, for he chose to present it during the class's daily sharing session. Again, when Skip read "Songs" to the class, he sang un-self-consciously. His classmates were appreciative, and commented on what they liked about the song. Matt particularly appreciated the rhythm, declaring, "I like the way you got the beat, like the mustache song we sang." Skip has songs humming in his mind, and, fortunately, he also has the freedom to take risks, share them with an audience, and even try to capture them on paper.

From a very young age, children sing and pantomime, scribble and draw, attempting to give shape to what they see, hear, and feel. The features of their environment reshape the ways that they use and organize their thought processes. The inventiveness in classroom environments that nurture children's creativity also points to another feature integral to helping children build on their potential: a recognition and acceptance of the diversity of ways of making meaning. These classrooms overflow with paints and brushes as well as pencils and pens, musical instruments as well as computers, and drama and dance as modes of communication as important as written work.

The children in these classes have taught me the importance of allowing them to experiment with a range of media and modes of expression. My fieldnotes are filled with vignettes that inform me of the children's thinking processes as they work, as the following example shows.

Excerpt from Fieldnotes, October 20, 1993

(Side by side, Maria and Charles sit by the window, their writing and drawing tools spread out before them as they create their stories. Charles puts down his pencil, turns to Maria, shuffles his papers, and asks, "Can I read you what I got?" When she nods her head, he begins: "One sunny day in the desert, two workers were digging up dinosaur bones. Finally the time came for them to go home. When they got home, they had a cup of cocoa and went to bed." As he turns to go on to the next page, he points to the drawing and casually informs Maria, "See, it's like I sliced the earth in half so you can see inside." Intrigued with this reference to his drawing, I pull my chair closer to Maria and Charles, turn on the tape recorder, and ask Charles to explain the drawing (Figure 8.1) to me, too.)

RUTH: You just told us [the drawing] is like a slice . . . of what?

CHARLES: It's like a . . . I sliced the sun in half, you see the lava, you can see the clouds real puffy? . . . and I drew it so the workers . . . so you could see inside the ground. And you can see the cactus roots and they were curling around the bone, and you know how some people would draw it where it would go right over the top?

RUTH: Mmm-hmm.

CHARLES: Well, what you do is, you stop there, and then go to the other side 'cause then it really does look like it's goin' around.

RUTH: Oh, you're right.

CHARLES: Joseph taught me that when he was drawing a Saturn.

RUTH: And what else is happening under the ground here?

CHARLES: Well, there's a claw right here, and there's a tooth, and there's two other teeth and there's a skull and the worker's also trying to get this skull, which is the head of a tyrannosaurus rex.

Figure 8.1   Excerpt from Charles's story

RUTH: So they think there might be a tyrannosaurus rex there? That's what they're trying to get to? Or do they not have any idea?

CHARLES: They don't have *any* idea. They're just sort of digging—trying to see if they can find one.

Charles's explanation continued for several more minutes, with the next two pages of his story and the accompanying drawings. Charles was not random in the choices that he made as he planned, organized, wrote, and drew his story. Like the other children I have observed and interviewed, his thinking processes are complex and interwoven. He has mapped out a great deal of the story itself, he's chosen a way to represent the earth so we readers can see what the workers in the story can't, and he's even gone to the trouble of trying to make the root wind around the bone, a strategy he is aware that he learned from Joseph—a year ago! He knows he can use whatever means are at his disposal in order to plan and communicate his meaning.

Human representation—and communication—of knowledge requires some kind of symbol system, or set of signs (Langer 1942; Goodman 1978;

Harste, Woodward, and Burke 1984; Vygotsky 1986). Our ideas may take form in images, movement, inner speech, mathematical symbols. We need a medium in which our ideas can take shape, but there is not just one medium: productive thought does not follow a uniform pattern.

Different cultures may embrace one symbol system above others and thus influence all the other systems as a child acquires communication and thinking skills. In some cultures, children are both instructed and cared for a great deal by touch as well as by word. They are carried on their mothers' or other caregivers' backs, incorporated into the rhythm of adult daily activities, and thus able to observe their world from many different angles and perspectives. In most industrialized societies, children become more dependent on verbal language, as they spend much of their early life in cribs and playpens, separated from more of their caregivers' physical cues. This pattern is carried over into schools, where the voice of the teacher is often the main mode of instruction and children are encouraged to build their communication skills largely through the spoken or written word.

In her study of what she calls the "inner languages" of thought, Vera John-Steiner (1985) concludes that our meanings are stored and organized differently depending on early internal modes of representation. We tend to develop a reliance on particular ways of learning, and these are patterned after the larger culture of which we are a part. We are also influenced by the home and, later, school environments. A steady diet of one kind of instruction shapes children's representations of thought far more narrowly than what is possible for them. Because other modalities are not encouraged to grow, the children's naturally rich ways of planning, solving problems, and storing memories can fade through disuse and lack of encouragement.

In the classrooms I have studied and worked in, there is a great diversity in children's thinking strategies. The children are not expected to check their cultures and their home lives at the classroom door. Instead, they are encouraged to build on their strengths, share their strategies with others, and learn different ways of thinking and communicating from their classmates and teachers. Though many children have a preferred mode of representation, they also learn a respect for different creative processes. They learn how other children think musically, mathematically, with their bodies, with pictures, or with words—and they learn to switch from one mode to another, often depending on the task at hand.

What do the different ways of organizing and communicating thought look like in different children? In the following section, I show some of the varied ways that children approach their work, drawing on their particular preferences.

INDIVIDUAL CHILDREN AND THEIR MODES
OF THINKING

 Jenna leans over her paper and adds branches to the tree she is drawing, then starts on a figure. She explains as she works, "The boy is looking up at the tree. 'Should we go in the tree? Do we dare, or . . . ?' This story will have dialogue."

"What made you decide to have dialogue?" I ask.

"I like to have dialogue. It helps other people find out what people are thinking. They'll understand the story better. Usually, I think of a high-pitched girl's voice and a little lower for a boy."

"Hmm. Do you hear these in your head?"

Jenna shakes her head. "Usually, I think of thoughts as silent. When I'm reading somebody else's book, I see in my head whatever they're writing about. If they're describing it, I can see it better and better. Thought can float, you know? I think of them as silent."

Though not all children are as articulate as Jenna, my interviews with children are peppered with references to hearing, or not hearing, voices in their minds. First graders Paul and Helen, from Pat McLure's class, offered these comments:

PAUL: You know how on funnies they're talking? I'm doing that. (*He draws a word bubble coming out of his character's mouth.*)

RUTH: Do you hear them talking as you write?

PAUL: Not really, but I can hear things in my head.

(*Helen shows me her piece about sharing her adventure story.*)

HELEN: That's Moira saying, "What was that supposed to say?" When I thought about that at home, it just sounded like Moira.

RUTH: Do you hear yourself in your head?

HELEN (*looks at me as though I'm crazy*):   My ears hear myself, not my head. I can hear the way Moira says it in my head. I could hear it tonight in my head without my ears, but not my own voice.

Contrast those comments with Matthew, a student in Leslie Funkhouser's class. His mental world is filled with sound, rather than the pictures that Jenna described. One morning, Matthew told me about the book he was reading, an exciting fantasy about a boy who turned into a television set. When I asked him how he pictured the boy in the story, he looked puzzled. He shrugged, "I guess he must look like me."

I asked him to close his eyes, then continued, "What do you see when you think of this book?"

Matthew waited a few seconds, then, with his eyes closed, shrugged again. "Black." He continued apologetically, "Sometimes I see pictures, but mostly I like hear it. I read, like, 'da-da-da,' but in my mind I hear it. I hear their words with the right tone of voice—not my voice—their voices."

Matthew's inner voice is important in his writing, too. He told me he needs to put word bubbles in his illustrations to show what his characters are saying. In a fictional piece called *Mr. Frog,* he felt his published book was lifeless until he added the sound to the illustrations. As he expressed it, "If you don't have the sound of what the snake and frog were saying or '*sss*-ing' or whatever, it's boring. It's just not like I imagined it." And in one story that he wrote about a skiing trip, he explained that "as I went over a jump, I was going, 'Hey, Ma, look!' so I put that in a word bubble.'"

Children internalize their social dialogue; this inner speech becomes the basis of their verbal thinking (Vygotsky 1978; 1986). For some children, such as Matthew, words are the primary way they represent the world to themselves. Matthew doesn't rely only on the convention of word bubbles to supply the sound he wants to his pieces of writing: his inner speech is often reported in the form of a monologue. In one such piece, the main character, "Detektiv Matthew," tells his story:

> I lookt all ofer town. I sad to myself now If I wer a dog were wold I hiyd Iv got It. Iv seyn lots of dogs in the aley downtown maybe that's war she is Iyl go look. I dont belev it ther are over 1000 dogs and not one is christey.

Other children could identify with Matthew when one day he talked about his "voices." Ilana told us the Care Bears talk to her as she writes about them, and "they have nice, friendly voices." Kristy is even aware of her inner voice as she writes: "I think, 'Well, maybe I should write this,' like I'm talking to myself." And when I read Matthew a quote from novelist Margaret Drabble, who reported, "I can hear all my sentences being said. I can hear them in my head to a marked extent," he smiled (John-Steiner 1985). "You took the words right outa my mouth!" he exclaimed.

For some children, the visual aspects of learning are paramount. Eight-year-old Kevin's inner representations were far more likely to deal with images, based on the keen observations that he made of the world around him. One morning when we were all making birthday cards for Isaac, Kevin decided his birthday greeting would be a baseball story with Isaac hitting a home run. His story is complete, captured on just one page to which he has given a kind of three-dimensionality (see Figure 8.2). Kevin made deliberate choices in his drawing that reflect the observations he had made recently at a

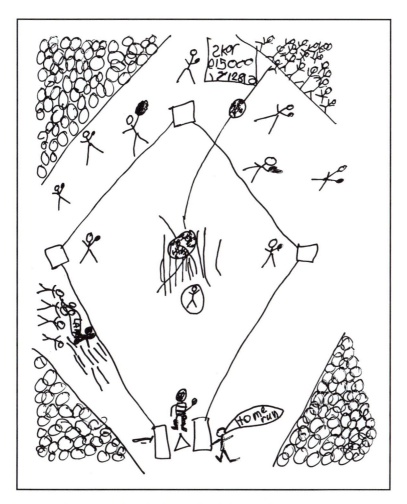

Figure 8.2   Kevin's baseball story birthday card

local Beavers baseball game. For example, he pointed out to me that he only made one corner of the spectator section standing. "They're standing up 'cause they're trying to catch the ball. I just went to a Beavers game—and only the people in the part that could catch it stood up."

Kevin also took pains to show the movement of the ball as it coursed through the air. "The ball's coming toward them," he explained, pointing to the crowd standing up in the right-hand corner of the drawing. "The ball is big 'cause it's closer, then it gets smaller as it goes down, down, down . . . I think I'm gonna make the ball a pop-up!" Kevin also uses the convention of "action lines" to show the movement of the ball—and Isaac's running, too.

Even the placement of the players on the field is intentional; Kevin named each position to me and the reasons for where they were standing. Though most of the players are stick figures, Kevin took more pains with the catcher, who is closest to the viewer. "I'll do the catcher the most detailed," he commented as he continued to draw. "Chest thing, knee pads . . ." As he viewed and re-viewed the images in his mind, he recorded them on the page. The only words he used in his baseball story were the words of Isaac's cheering fans screaming, "Go, Isaac," and the umpire shouting, "Home run!"

Kevin reminded me of another author who made conscious use of images in his writing, C. S. Forester, who reflected:

> Sitting at a writing table writing words on paper, what is it that forms these words? What is going on in my mind as I write them? I have no doubt that in my case it is a matter of a series of visualizations. Not two-dimensional, as if looking at a television screen; three-dimensional, perhaps, as if I were a thin, thin, invisible ghost walking about on a stage while a play is in actual performance. (1964, p. 123)

Just as some children, like Matthew, are sensitive to the ways others use sound to communicate information, Kevin notices how people use images to tell stories. He is particularly interested in wordless picture books, poring over books like *The Silver Pony: A Story in Pictures* (Ward 1973), and often choosing books with the conventions that appear in comics and cartoons. In his own stories, it is often the pictures that tell the story, with the words there to elaborate on the context, with knocks at the door, slamming, gulping, exploding, or cheering added later.

Other children who rely on observation and visual thinking find the constraints of a page too restrictive. The conventions that Kevin uses, like the action lines, the multiple drawings of an object, and even pop-ups, don't create the flow of action that matches the movie-like images in their minds. Maria experimented with bringing her adventure beyond the edges of a page. One of her stories was about a little girl and her teacher, Jill. The first two pages were large drawings that introduced the main character and the setting, with the captions: "Jill iz a nois Tech" and "Jill went in a Bot."

"I'm gonna tape these together, so it can be like a film," she explained to me. And that's exactly what she did, taping the consecutive pages into a long string of "film," then looping it through the back of a chair so that the picture in front of the chair resembled a screen. Calling a group of children to see her story, she sat them down on the floor and pulled the long strip of paper through the chair as she read each page.

Many other children use their bodies to search for information and knowledge, and to communicate it. Some, like Jaime, rely heavily on their arms and legs—on movement—in their creative processes. When Jaime writes, and talks about writing, he relies on gesture. When he wrote his story about karate, he didn't picture the moves, he acted them out, looked at his body position, then drew the pictures. The procedure was interesting to watch. That morning, he sat at his desk thinking for several moments, and although he was lost in thought, he seemed to jerk his head as he pondered. Finally, he took his writing folder and retreated to a table in the back of the room. After setting everything on the table, he gave a powerful kick to the side, then froze. He looked down at his extended leg and the angle of his foot, reflected for a moment, then drew a picture. Under the picture, he wrote, "This is a side blade kick." He continued that morning and several subsequent mornings to execute, then draw and label several karate kicks and blocks.

When Jaime tells his stories, or explains how he works on projects, he tends to act it out, using his hands to stir the air, for example, when he talks about cooking. Rudolf Arnheim contends that people can sharpen mental images and focus thinking by simplifying them into an expressive gesture or posture. "Thoughts need shape, and shape must be derived from some medium," he writes (1969, p. 116). For some children, like Jaime, that medium is gesture.

Most of the children I have observed tended to have a preferred mode of thinking and expression. This is in keeping with Howard Gardner's theories of multiple intelligence (1991). Gardner's work suggests that people are capable of at least seven different ways of knowing the world, which he has labeled as distinct *intelligences*. He states that

> We are all able to know the world through language, logical-mathematical analysis, spatial representation, musical thinking, the use of the body to solve problems or to make things, an understanding of other individuals, and an understanding of ourselves. Where individuals differ is in the strength of these intelligences . . . and in the ways in which such intelligences are invoked and combined to carry out different tasks, solve diverse problems, and progress in various domains. (p. 12)

Another psychologist, Jerome Kagan, has done similar work in the field of domains of personality. He believes that all of us are born with what he calls a "personality bias": it might be toward shyness or assertiveness, for example, or toward a more active or passive nature (Kagan 1987). These personality traits are tempered and shaped by the culture and environment to which we are exposed.

Combining aspects of Gardner's and Kagan's theories with my own observations, I believe we are also born with a "cognitive bias" in terms of our modes of thinking as well as with personality traits—not as popular psychology would have it, in terms of right-brained or left-brained thinking, but along a continuum, where some of us tend to rely more on one mode or another, or organize our thoughts through one particular medium more strongly than others.

Besides a natural bias toward a strategy, children also take into account the task they are working on. In Jill's classroom, Tara often found ways to incorporate her inclination toward music, such as researching the folk songs of the Civil War era. After her performance of a play on the life of Harriet Tubman, she taught all the children the song "Follow the Drinking Gourd," which she had woven into her presentation. Yet when Tara designed and planned a garden with her partner, she relied on her mathematical thinking strategies for estimating and measuring, as well as detailed drawings of the flowers, vegetables, and herbs she wanted to plant. Her strength as a musical thinker did not serve this task as well, so she relied on other abilities, continuing to hone them as she worked.

In Pat McLure's classroom, I found children often relied on different intelligences, depending on the work in which they were involved. If a child could best express the motion of waves through drawings and pop-ups, for example, then she would rely on a more pictorial representation of her story about the ocean (Hubbard 1989). The same child, though, on another day might write out detailed conversations of an interview she had conducted with no drawings as part of her communication. Findings such as these point out the fallacies of the old learning styles debates, where students were labeled as learners in one mode or another, then taught according their supposed strengths, or sometimes "remediated" into a preferable mode of thinking.

In order to have different learning tools at their disposal, though, so that they can make choices depending on what they hope to accomplish, children need to have experience with a range of possibilities. What is key is to help children realize that many modalities of thought are available. Each of us might find a preference, but what encourages novel thought is exploring ways that these modalities can work together, and how we can switch from one to another as our tasks and problems change.

Problem solving itself tends to be framed by the way our thinking is organized. To paraphrase Abraham Maslow, if the only tool you know how to use is a hammer, you tend to see the problems of the world as a series of nails. So, when we are presented with new, messy, real-world problems, we are likely to frame them by strategies we have in our mental repertoire. Our experience with a range of modalities has an enormous impact on our capacity for creative thought.

PROBLEM POSING

 Problem posing works in concert with our different modes of thinking; we frame our problems in the ways we are able to see possibilities within the structure of our minds. Rather than being problem
solvers, creative thinkers are first and foremost *problem finders* who are able
to frame their queries to begin their quests. We need to move away from the
kinds of neat and tidy problems with teacher-edition answers to the messy
problems that articulate real-world dilemmas, so that children can explore a
diversity of thinking modalities in the midst of genuine inquiry.

Teacher-researcher Magdalene Lampert's work is one example of the ways
that we can help students build on their abilities to pose problems. In her
fifth-grade classroom, she approached mathematics as a discipline where
"together they learn to raise questions, put forth hypotheses about underlying principles, and explore the whole arena of mathematical understanding"
(1990, p. 32). Rather than looking for correct answers, students in Lampert's
classroom engaged in mathematical conversations. Lampert reports that this
involved the students' noticing—and questioning—the meanings in patterns,
defining issues, taking risks in their thinking, making choices.

The issues involved in mathematical problem posing are clearly relevant
in other areas of the curriculum. As writers, historians, artists—in all areas—
children need to rely on themselves as the most important problem posers.
When learners work on projects—in groups, as well as individually—they
have an opportunity to examine the structure of the problem they are pursu-
ing. The feasibility of different avenues must be considered, choices made
and pursued. The whole world of problem solving and the joys of research
come into play.

Think of the important thinking and problem posing that is involved in
project-based classrooms on a daily basis. In Jill Ostrow's classroom, I was
witness to creative thinking in action as the children worked on their
research into the Inuit culture. On this morning, Jill called them together in
the meeting area and asked them, "How will you share with an audience
what you have learned?" The range of possible demonstrations the children
chose was astounding: plays, puppet shows, hypercard, models, paintings,
songs—and yes, even written stories. Each choice set in motion a whole
chain of problems the children would need to first pose, then solve, as they
worked to present their findings in their chosen modes.

Jill explained her philosophy to the parents in this way:

> What I have learned from watching the children work is phenomenal! I have
> discovered that a "problem" is not . . . "There are two frogs and two more

came, how many in all?" A problem is just that: a *problem!* Something that takes thought, organization, mistakes and fixing or using mistakes, sharing, teaching, and learning. A problem poses a challenge—something they can't solve, but need to work out. These problems include math, writing, reading, science, cooperative learning, and presentation. I am *so* excited not only by the end results, but much more, by the thinking process each child went through. (excerpt from May 1993 newsletter to parents)

BUILDING BRIDGES: WORKING ON A REAL PROBLEM

Inventive environments such as Jill's classroom give learners the creative experience they need—experience asking genuine questions and exploring a range of novel solutions. Over the course of a year, Jill's students work on several real problems that allow them to explore options, using their cognitive biases as well as taking risks and exploring other possibilities.

An extended project that the children in Jill's class worked on one year involved designing and building bridges. This project can serve as a kind of case study of what it looks like when children of different ages, strengths, and diverse ways of making meaning collaborate on a genuine real-world problem. The work the children did on this project also points out that some of their individual cognitive biases may not be particularly helpful for the task at hand. In addition, not every intelligence or modality is represented in this project. Artificially incorporating music, for example, into bridge building trivializes both music as a genuine way of making meaning, and the reality of the task at hand.

The bridge-building problem grew out of a classroom interest raised by the children. In the island community that they had formed, the Planning Committee decided that the room really needed a bridge to get from one part of their island classroom to another. Stephanie, one of the members of this committee, brought the idea to the whole class, and they decided to pursue the project.

Jill's role as teacher was crucial. Though she would be a learner with them in terms of actual bridge construction, she was an important resource. The next day, she brought in all the books the library had on bridges, with picture books, atlases of bridges from around the world, stories about bridge construction. She also encouraged the children to bring in their funds of knowledge, since the nearest city—Portland, Oregon—is divided by the Willamette River and connected by eight bridges. Some, though not all, of the children remembered crossing the bridges, either on the footpaths to watch parades, or riding in cars or buses, and they shared what they remembered from these excursions.

Jill decided to expand their knowledge of bridges with a combination of books, pictures, and hands-on experiences that would incorporate a study of physical structures, area, and volume. She expected the children to explore different kinds of materials and ultimately plan and build their own bridges, using whatever materials worked best for them. In order to get them thinking from the start of bridges as three-dimensional constructions, Jill asked the children to begin by making a simple bridge out of clay, then drawing their bridges so that they could see ways the actual physical entity might be represented on paper for future plans.

Stephanie brought her drawing to the whole-class meeting, showing how she drew her bridge from two different perspectives, both a side and a top view. She also noted that the clay was "easy to work with." This double perspective idea spread through the class like wildfire; soon not only Stephanie but Marek, Tara, and Joseph drew their bridges from two perspectives.

Stephanie's introduction of the vocabulary of perspective and the notion of recording on paper two different views helped reinforce the notion that the students' bridges and plans could show a three-dimensional structure. Based on what she had assessed from their first bridge attempts in clay, Jill next asked them to experiment with different materials—and more detailed plans.

After showing the children more pictures of bridges, she closed the session by holding up pictures of the Golden Gate Bridge, including the plans for building it. "OK," she concluded. "Here are the materials for you to try another bridge: a piece of cardboard, string, tape, and scissors. The string needs to stay on the table. When you go with a partner, take one piece." She issued a challenge for this new bridge: "The bridge you make with these materials has to open like this . . . or like this." (Jill demonstrated a bridge opening with her hands). "You have lots of time to figure this out. Some of you will want to sit and think first, and others will want to start right away. Kevin? Who do you want for a partner?"

The children chose partners and set to work. Because of the flexible predictability of their classroom structure, they knew they had access to their own processes of working: the materials, the collaborators, and the supportive environment. Jill had set that structure in place (see insert page 4).

As the kids worked, I talked with them and watched their several solutions. During recess, I listed the skills I had noticed them use in just one hour:

- problem solving
- problem posing
- measuring
- planning

- designing
- writing
- revising
- drawing
- listing
- evaluating
- reflecting
- negotiating (as part of collaboration)
- exhibiting
- explaining
- using spatial (3-D) thinking

Within the writing, designing, revising, I saw a great deal of risk taking and learning from mistakes. In addition, the children showed high tolerance for a range of possibilities rather than one narrow solution, an ability to work with sustained effort for an hour (so much for kids' supposed short attention spans!) and a lot of enjoyment and playfulness, with boats going under the bridges, satellite towers jutting into the sky, fish darting about in the water.

What I didn't observe is important, too: I didn't hear anyone say, "This is too hard" or "I can't do this" or "She stole my idea" or "I can't work with him" or "Mine is better than yours." We saw a room full of cooperating, thinking, motivated, creative people.

As the project progressed, Jill encouraged her students' risk taking and experimentation, bringing in a variety of new materials, including pins, straws, popsicle sticks, string, tape, toilet paper tubes, and poster board (see insert page 4). They read books together, brought in stories and accounts of their personal experiences with bridges, and organized a field trip to go to Portland and ride down the river under the bridges so they could see bridge construction from a different angle, as well as compare the way the different bridges looked. Throughout the whole process, they kept records of their plans and designs, of what they learned and what they observed. This helped give Jill and me insights into the strategies that the different children employed.

Maria and Fiona relied very much on hands-on physical exploration, learning as they tried out different patterns. They first built a structure with blocks, then carefully drew that in order to help them figure out how to make the same structure with other materials.

Micah drew a picture of the materials he would need, with arrows to explain how and where they would be used. Lisa relied on combinations of words and pictures in her plan for a suspension bridge. Spencer relied largely on written reflections and mathematical manipulations to modify his plans as they continued to take shape, as his "Bridge Reflection" exemplifies:

We changed the road from a foot to 8 inches and instead of gluing the pop-sicles sticks together, then glue X's under the road, we glued X's to hold the road together. Now, our bridge is 8 inches long and 4 inches wide.

The children's reflections show the many options that were available to them for recording their inner designs. Some children relied largely on ver-bal thinking and recording. Eight-year-old Stephanie reflected on the field trip by sitting down at the computer and writing the following:

My class went on a felled trip,
to look at bridges. We sow the Fremond Bridg and the Marcm bridg, the Hothorn Bridg, the Ross Island Bridg, the Morrison Bridg, the Steel Bridg, the Brodway Bridg. We allso sow lots of sips, the strongest thing that hollds bridges up is, x's and triagels. A triagel is a extremle stronog sape. "Oh" I for-got to tell you that we were on a ship that is called the Rose. The river that we went on was the Wulamet river. We ate on the bout,
it was fun.
"Oh" I forgot to say we so the brunside bridg.

Now let's touk abawt what I lurnd!

the Hothorn bridg opens, the Steel bridg opens and the Burnside bridg opens, put there is lots more bridges that open.
the oldest bridg is the Burnside bridg, and the seckent oldest is the Hothorn bridg. they are well over 100 yers old but the Hothorn mite be a little under 100 yers old, I do not no!

Six-year-old Tegan used a similar process, writing about what she saw, and later adding small pictures at the bottom to illustrate her work (Fig-ure 8.3). But the message is clear enough with just her words:

We went under 8 bridges. The Sellwood Bridge is the oldest bridge in Port-land. The Broadway Bridge is the second oldest in Portland.

Other children relied much more on the mental images that they saw. Molly, for example, made a drawing from the perspective of the bridge from underneath (Figure 8.4). She even showed what a car driving over the bridge looked like from that angle. Her caption reads, "This is the Hawthorne Bridge and it does open up."
Nolan's reliance on keen observation and a combination of mathematical and visual thinking is clear in his reflection:

They have triangles and rectangles and hexagons. They use beams on the bot-tom of the bridge to hold the bridge up.

For their culminating project, the children, individually or with partners, were to create bridges using any combination of materials they wanted. The

Figure 8.3   Tegan's reflection on the field trip

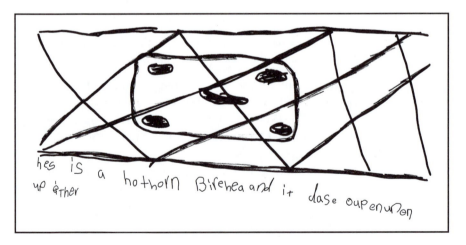

Figure 8.4   Molly's perspective drawing

challenge that Jill set before them was that the bridges would need to be structurally sound, able to hold weight. This would require careful, well-thought-out plans; the children would have to think ahead, frame their projects, and pose problems that needed to be solved.

But they didn't work in isolation; as their bridge plans and construction progressed, they continued to meet as a group and share what was working and what wasn't, offering support and advice to each other:

Excerpt from Fieldnotes, December 8, 1993

(The class is gathered at the platform area. Jill asks them what problems they are having as they design and build their bridges.)

LISA: Our supports keep coming down. The toilet rolls bent.

JENNA: You could put sticks in.

MOLLY: Maybe the rolls are too heavy for the support. Could you add another support?

PAUL: You could put clay inside.

MOLLY: Ours kept collapsing in, so we put popsicle sticks in for more support.

MICAH: We made the other triangle, but we haven't put it together yet.

PAUL: Maybe you could use something stronger instead of paper—popsicle sticks and string.

The children are learning that they have myriad resources as they pose and solve problems. They can turn to each other and learn from the experiments that a friend is making, even though they may be using different materials. They learn the fluidity of the creative process, too—that designs and plans are important, but that plans are not set in stone and may require substantial revision.

Spiraling back to earlier learning is another vital aspect of creative thought and development. Anthropologist Mary Catherine Bateson calls people capable of transferring experiences from one cycle to another, shifting gears and starting again in this way, "zigzag people." "A zigzag," she writes, "seen from another angle, may be a rising spiral, so that readjustments are not a record of failure, but of growth" (1994, p. 82).

Children need that record of growth to refer back to, delineating the journey. Just as it provided insights for Jill and me, it provided valuable reflection for the children themselves into their processes. Jill consciously builds this reflection into their work. For example, after sharing their difficulties and the problems they were solving, the children returned to their "bridge folders" and wrote how they would proceed to address the difficulties they were experiencing. Stephanie used graph paper to redesign the bridge she and Lisa were constructing. She wrote, "As you can see, we put popsicle sticks on, and we put one more tube on. And now it's not going to open, because the string was not holding up. So, that's why we put popsicle sticks and one more tube on."

The zigzagging, spiraling back, planning, doing, revising, all feed into the projects and problems that the children work on. It is also important for children to share their strategies with others. The children benefited from our discussions of thought processes. They often tried each others' strategies—modifying them, adopting them, discarding them if they were not helpful. This caused them to consciously reflect on the choices that they made.

Classrooms can best suit students' creative needs when they are set up so that each child's unique strategies and modes of thinking will be fostered, rather than narrowly channeled in one direction. Whether the children are building bridges, learning about the Civil War, or exploring the Arctic, they know that a range of possibilities for exploration and exhibition are possible. They also know that some projects will be more difficult for them than others. Children like Stephanie and Nolan were natural leaders in the bridge-building project, while Jenna and Molly turned to ways of solving problems that they hadn't tried before and needed to rely on classmates to help build those skills. Their role as leaders emerges in other long-term projects. For example, as I write (at the end of the 1994–95 school year), the children are producing an end-of-the-year musical to present to the school, explaining the places they've been in their time travel machine. Jenna has been conducting mini-classes on musical notation, and Molly is the producer-director. This project requires skills and cognitive biases different from those important for bridge building.

All of their projects require planning, problem posing, and ultimately problem solving. A world of possibilities is open to the children when they are in environments that provide the tools that expand their thinking repertoires rather than narrow their options. In looking back over the bridge project, I find it hard to separate the different strategies the children used because they became so interdependent. They thought with their bodies, with mathematical concepts, with images, and with words. They took on the roles of construction workers, of planning commissioners, of city tourists. And their attention was reshaped by the stimuli that were part of their social environment, enriching their capacity to search and learn.

Children are hard at work—selecting, condensing, and interpreting their impressions. They have varied inner processes and patterns of thought, which they use to give shape to what they see, hear, and imagine. It is our responsibility to set up classrooms that aid them in their pursuit of knowledge by helping them make the most of their own unique inner designs, and so encourage them to constantly expand and enlarge their possibilities.

9

A Workshop of the Possible

Lewis Carroll wrote a fantasy about a lock that runs around in distress, crying, "I'm looking for someone to unlock me." The children we meet in our schoolrooms every day need someone in their lives who will help unlock the talents that are within them. They need caring, creative adults who believe in each child's considerable abilities. But they also need resources, skills, and self-confidence in their own creative abilities to find those keys themselves.

The situations in which children will continue to find themselves as learners throughout life will not remain the same. Change is inevitable. The most important invisible keys we can help our children forge are the abilities to build on what they know and improvise in new situations, reflecting on their knowledge so that it is in the architecture of their memories. When these abilities become part of their repertoire, they will be able to use the knowledge and strategies again, in whatever unpredictable situations that may arise. We need to help children learn by broadening our goals for them rather than narrowing them down into single outcomes. We need to treat children and their creative abilities with greater respect.

Treating children with respect means treating them as *whole people*, people who are looking for meaning in what they do and who have many different ways to learn. They need to be involved in meaningful, substantial work, expected to solve problems and grapple with ideas that are compelling. The stories presented in these pages of creative learners, whether experienced adults or young children, speak strongly for the need to stress curriculum that is both meaningful and context-based. Unfortunately, for most school learning, this is still not the case. Catherine Lewis and her colleagues surveyed

United States schools' curriculum in 1995 and found it was largely created without the long-term goal of genuine, meaningful, and substantial work for children:

> Most curriculum in United States schools is determined by default—by textbook publishers and standardized tests that create a de facto national curriculum of isolated facts and subskills. The dispositions that are so central to a democratic productive society—such personal qualities as fairness, a desire to contribute to society's betterment, a capacity to relate to diverse others, a willingness to work hard, a desire to learn—are noticeably absent from this curriculum, despite the widespread recognition of their importance. (Lewis, Schaps, and Watson 1995, p. 550)

If our goal is to help children become lifelong learners, as opposed to memorizers of "isolated facts and subskills," it is vital that the curriculum in classrooms be intrinsically worth learning and academically challenging. One of the themes that occurs again and again in the curriculum that the teachers created with their students in the classrooms I investigated is the centrality of children as researchers. Their natural abilities to observe, question, and look for meaning and patterns can—and, I believe, should—be at the heart of curriculum building, along with opportunities to hone these abilities and add new skills in the process of improvising in ever-changing research situations.

CHILDREN AS RESEARCHERS

Children come to school with questions, with five years of experience noticing, trying to understand and explain their world. Though they don't stop asking those questions when they come to school, they often learn that school isn't the place to pursue their answers. But children's insights and questions clearly *can* become part of the curriculum, even though the questions the children have are as diverse as their backgrounds, interests, and experiences. In a flexible working environment, a six-year-old child like Fiona can pursue her questions and fascination with rabbits, discovering answers to such questions as: "Do rabbits live in families like we do?" and "How big are rabbits when they are born?" In the same classroom, there is space for eight-year-old Tara to explore her question: "What holds bubbles together?" And seven-year-old Jeremy can find out how the color in comic books gets printed. Their teacher sees a major part of her role as helping children explore these questions as part of their daily work. Examples of children exploring their wonderings in inquiry models are becoming more widespread—but they need to be more common still (Boomer 1992; Short and Burke 1991).

We have seen the power and possibility of students collaborating on whole-class research inquiries, too: from hands-on research into the structure of bridges to observing and documenting the life cycle of butterflies to answering student-generated questions about the Arctic. This research adds to the curriculum the important dimension of working together on larger community goals, apprenticing children to each other and to a variety of mentors. It also allows children to see that there are various ways to tackle an issue or a problem, that they can choose to work from their own particular strengths while gaining exposure to the processes of others.

Children's need to answer their questions and reflect on their learning comes together when their skills as researchers are respected, refined, and expanded—such skills as posing questions and finding problems, experimenting with framing the problems in new and untried ways, delighting in the risks and possibilities the new ways may open. Curriculum can grow from helping children gain experience with their ability to make detailed observations, including ways to nudge them to try out a multitude of recording and sharing techniques. Even very young children can learn to find information from books and distant teachers, as Maria did when she studied chimps and investigated the methodologies of Jane Goodall, or when Fiona delighted in the triumphs and techniques of Georgia O'Keeffe.

When children are immersed daily in research, they are capable of insights into the process that come to many of us only in adulthood. When Micah was explaining one page of his research to me, he confided: "The thing about research questions is, you keep doing the research and you have more and more questions!" Even more exciting than Micah's insight is his comfortable stance toward ambiguity that his statement implies, and his understanding and acceptance of the generative nature of research and quests for knowledge.

Young children's creative abilities show up clearly when they are in environments that honor their capacity for research, reflection, and improvisation. Rather than continue to believe that there are only a few "gifted and talented" individuals who don't fit in with our preexisting child development theories, we need to reevaluate old theories that do not fit with what we are learning about children.

REEVALUATING WHAT CHILDREN CAN DO

In attending deeply to children and trying to empathize with them, as in studying other cultures, one is constantly reminded that these beloved strangers are behaving in ways that are only intelligible if their world is recognized as differently structured, laid out according to different landmarks. Much of the time we are busy trying to talk children out of their perceptions, giving them the correct answers, the ones that are widely shared and fit neatly into familiar systems of interpretation.

MARY CATHERINE BATESON

The vignettes from the classroom presented in this book and the interviews with children in the midst of their creative endeavors show their extraordinary abilities. These examples support a body of work that has not yet become part of mainstream educational theory but is vital to consider as we work to construct environments that nurture children's creative capabilities. To be blunt, it's time to move beyond Piaget.

Jean Piaget remains the most cited child developmentalist. Yet important work by post-Piagetians show that Piaget was wrong in believing that young children cannot engage in logical thought (Sameroff and McDonough 1994). Rochel Gelman and Renee Baillargeon conclude:

> What Piaget had seen as new intellectual breakthroughs by the 5- to 7-year-old child were already within the capacity of much younger children and were perhaps even innate. Complex understanding of number concepts, spatial transformation, and causality could be found in pre-schoolers and even in infants. (1983, p. 167)

Furthermore, Piaget ignored elements of the environment that influence development and changes in thought. We must look more closely at the effect of children's experiences in the family, in the community, and in the classroom. Vera John-Steiner's pioneering work in the development of creative thinkers shows the impact of their early environments in developing preferences for certain ways of knowing and for developing important invisible tools to aid their thinking (see Chapter 8). Child developmentalist Barbara Rogoff takes this position a step further, stating that changes in children's abilities can be understood *only* in terms of their sociocultural activities (Rogoff 1993). Rogoff argues that

> The age when a child moves from one stage to another depends on the meaning and support given that transition in the life of the culture. One example is the age at which children begin to take care of other children. The major cognitive requirement for such a role is that the caregiver be able to assume the perspective of the younger child in order to understand the child's signals and ensure its well-being. In industrial societies, such perspective-taking is not found until after the 5- to 7-year shift, and children usually do not become babysitters until they are at least 10 years old. Among the Mayan villagers of Guatemala, 3- to 5-year olds are able to be babysitters because of the social

organization of family roles and cultural expectations of that community . . . [This] difference is to be found in the Mayan training of children to become interdependent members of the community, while children in the U.S. are encouraged to assert individuality and be competitive. (p. 192)

Early experiences also play an integral role in formation of memory structures. Changes in the ability to remember may be related to the extent to which memories are shared with others, according to Katherine Nelson (1993): "Pre-school children do not remember specific events for long periods of time *unless* they have had the opportunity to talk about them with a parent or teacher . . . To the extent that parents and educators encourage narration, children's memory capacity may be precocious. To the extent that children are placed in passive roles in educational settings, memory and cognitive development may be delayed" (1993, p. 191).

The most important advice we can give educators and those who work with young children is to assume that children *are* developmentally able to learn. The teacher's job is to create an environment that is complex, stimulating, and interesting—and to work with the child to find the keys that will unlock that child's potential.

In Beverly Cleary's novel *Ramona the Brave* the seven-year-old heroine asks, "Why don't grown-ups know that children think important thoughts?" We need to remember that children do think important thoughts, and that they have strategies for learning, remembering, researching, imagining, collaborating. We need to encourage them to share their insights with us, to be active agents in the environment.

A WORKSHOP OF THE POSSIBLE

If we are truly to build on children's natural creative abilities, we need to create a workshop of the possible in our schools—a workshop where it is possible for children to explore their obsessions, take risks in their thinking, and apprentice themselves to many other learners; a workshop where there is a shift in the locus of control in the classroom from teacher to student, where students take more responsibility for the problems they choose to solve; a workshop where it is possible for children to create personal inventories of their knowledge and their stories, where they aren't expected to check their cultures at the door; a workshop where there is time for students to be the learners that they were born to be, and where we as teachers appreciate and delight in the extraordinary creative abilities of each child.

References

Professional Literature

Anderson, J. R. 1985. *Cognitive Psychology and Its Implications.* 2nd ed. New York: W. H. Freeman.

Arnheim, Rudolf. 1969. *Visual Thinking.* Berkeley, CA: University of California Press.

Atwell, Nancie. 1987. *In the Middle: Writing, Reading, and Learning with Adolescents.* Portsmouth, NH: Boynton/Cook.

———. 1994. "Re-Imagining Curriculum." Keynote Address delivered at Re-Imagining Curriculum Conference. Portland, Maine.

Austin, Terri. 1994. *Changing the View: Student-Led Parent Conferences.* Portsmouth, NH: Heinemann.

Barell, John. 1980. *Playgrounds of Our Minds.* New York: Teachers College Press.

Bateson, Mary Catherine. 1994. *Peripheral Visions: Learning Along the Way.* New York: HarperCollins.

Bayer, Ann. 1990. *Collaborative-apprenticeship Learning: Language and Thinking Across the Curriculum, K–12.* Mountain View, CA: Mayfield Publishing.

Boden, Margaret. 1991. *The Creative Mind: Myths and Mechanisms.* New York: Basic Books.

Boomer, Garth. 1992. "Curriculum Composing and Evaluating: An Invitation to Action Research." In *Negotiating the Curriculum: Educating for the 21st Century,* edited by Garth Boomer, Nancy Lester, Cynthia Onore, and Jon Cook. London: The Falmer Press.

Brown, A., and R. Ferrara. 1985. "Diagnosing Zones of Proximal Development." In *Cultural Communication and Cognition,* edited by Ann Brown. Cambridge, UK: Cambridge University Press.

Bruner, Jerome. 1984. "Language, Mind, and Reading." In *Awakening to Literacy,* edited by H. Goelman, A. Oberg, and F. Smith. Portsmouth, NH: Heinemann.

———. 1987. *Making Sense: The Child's Construction of the World.* New York: Methuen.

Calvin, William H., and George A. Ojemann. 1994. *Conversations with Neil's Brain: The Neural Nature of Thought and Language*. Reading, MA: Addison-Wesley.

Childs, C. P., and P. M. Greenfield. 1980. "Informal Modes of Learning and Teaching: The Case of Zinacanteco Learning." In *Studies in Cross-Cultural Psychology*, vol. 2, edited by N. Warren. New York: Academic Press.

Chomsky, Noam. 1965. *Aspects of the Theory of Syntax*. Cambridge, MA: M.I.T. Press.

Craik, F. I., and R. Lockhart. 1972. "Levels of Processing: A Framework for Memory Research." *Journal of Verbal Learning and Verbal Behavior* 11: 671–684.

Curtis, JoAnn. 1994. "Balance the Basics: Teaching and Learning." *Teacher Research: The Journal of Classroom Inquiry* 1, no. 2: 145–148.

Dewey, John. (1915) 1990. *The School and Society*. Rev. ed. Chicago: University of Chicago Press.

Doerr, Harriet. 1991. "A Sleeve of Rain." In *The Writer on Her Work: New Essays in New Territory*, vol. 2, edited by Janet Sternburg. New York: W. W. Norton.

Donaldson, Margaret. 1978. *Children's Minds*. New York: W. W. Norton.

Dudley-Marling, Curt, and Dennis Searle. 1991. *When Students Have Time to Talk: Creating Contexts for Learning Language*. Portsmouth, NH: Heinemann.

Ehrlich, Gretel. 1994. *A Match to the Heart*. New York: Pantheon.

Epel, Naomi. 1993. *Writer's Dreaming*. New York: Carol Southern Books.

Ernst, Karen. 1994. *Picturing Learning*. Portsmouth, NH: Heinemann.

Forester, C. S. 1964. *The Hornblower Companion*. Boston: Little, Brown.

Forman, Edward, and Courtney Cazden. 1985. "Exploring Vygotskian Perspectives in Education: The Cognitive Value of Peer Interaction." In *Culture, Communication, and Cognition: Vygotskian Perspectives*, edited by J. V. Wertsch. New York: Cambridge University Press.

Fueyo, Judith. 1991. "Reading 'Literate Sensibilities': Resisting a Verbocentric Writing Classroom." *Language Arts* 68: 641–648.

Gardner, Howard. 1983. *Frames of Mind: The Theory of Multiple Intelligences*. New York: Basic Books.

———. 1991. *The Unschooled Mind: How Children Think and How Schools Should Teach*. New York: Basic Books.

Gelman, Rochel, and Renee Baillargeon. 1983. "A Review of Some Piagetian Concepts." In *Handbook of Child Psychology*, vol. 3, edited by Paul H. Mussen. New York: Wiley.

Goldberg, Natalie. 1990. *Wild Mind: Living the Writer's Life*. New York: Bantam Books.

Goodfield, June. 1981. *An Imagined World: A Story of Scientific Discovery*. New York: Harper and Row.

Goodman, Kenneth. 1994. "Standards—Not!" In *The Council Chronicle* 4, no. 2: 20.

Goodman, Nelson. 1978. *Ways of Worldmaking*. Indianapolis, IN: Hackett.

Goodman, Yetta, and Kenneth Goodman. 1990. "Vygotsky in a Whole Language Perspective." In *Vygotsky and Education: Instructional Implications and Applications of Sociohistorical Psychology*, edited by L. Moll. New York: Cambridge University Press.

Gracey, Harry. 1967. "Learning the Student Role: Kindergarten as Academic Boot Camp." In *Sociology of Contemporary Society* 11: 243–254.

Graves, Donald. 1994. *A Fresh Look at Writing*. Portsmouth, NH: Heinemann.

Graves, Donald, and Jane Hansen, producers. 1986a. *One Classroom: A Child's View*. Written and edited by James Whitney, Ruth Hubbard, and Brenda Miller. Videotape No. 2 of the series *The Writing and Reading Process*. Portsmouth, NH: Heinemann.

———. 1986b. *Time and Choice: Key Elements for Process Teaching*. Written and edited by James Whitney and Ruth Hubbard. Videotape no. 1 of the series *The Writing and Reading Process*. Portsmouth, NH: Heinemann.

Hansen, Jane. 1987. *When Writers Read*. Portsmouth, NH: Heinemann.

Harste, Jerome, and Kathy Short, with Carolyn Burke. 1988. *Creating Classrooms for Authors: The Reading-Writing Connection*. Portsmouth, NH: Heinemann.

Harste, Jerome, Virginia Woodward, and Carolyn Burke. 1984. *Language Stories and Literacy Lessons*. Portsmouth, NH: Heinemann.

Holland, Norman. 1975. *Dynamics of Literary Response*. New York: W. W. Norton.

Horowitz, Michael. 1970. *Image Formation and Cognition*. New York: Appleton-Century-Crofts.

Hubbard, Ruth. 1986. "Structure Encourages Independence in Reading and Writing." In *The Reading Teacher*. November: vol. 40, 180–185.

———. 1989. *Authors of Pictures, Draughtsmen of Words*. Portsmouth, NH: Heinemann.

———. 1993. "Time Will Tell." In *Language Arts Journal*, November: vol. 70, no. 7, 574–582.

Jacobsen, Mary. 1982. "Looking for Literary Space: The Willing Suspension of Disbelief Re-visited." In *Research in the Teaching of English* 16: 21–38.

Johnson, George. 1991. *In the Palaces of Memory: How We Build the Worlds Inside Our Heads*. New York: Alfred A. Knopf.

Johnson, Robert. 1986. *Inner Work*. New York: Harper and Row.

John-Steiner, Vera. 1985. *Notebooks of the Mind: Explorations of Thinking*. Albuquerque, NM: University of New Mexico Press.

Kagan, Jerome. 1987. Videotape recording of University of New Hampshire Psychology Department Colloquia Series. Durham, NH: University of New Hampshire Psychology Department.

Kohn, Alfie. 1993. *Punished by Rewards: The Trouble with Gold Stars, Incentive Plans, A's, Praise, and Other Bribes*. Boston: Houghton Mifflin.

Laminack, Lester, and Sandra Lawing. 1994. "Building Generative Curriculum. In *Primary Voices K–6* 2, no. 3: 8–18.

Lampert, Magdalene. 1990. "When the Problem Is Not the Question and the Solution Is Not the Answer: Mathematical Knowing and Teaching." In *American Educational Research Journal* 27: 29–64.

Langer, Suzanne. 1942. *Philosophy in a New Key*. Cambridge, MA: Harvard University Press.

Lepper, Mark, David Greene, and Richard Nisbett. 1973. "Undermining Children's Intrinsic Interest with Extrinsic Rewards." In *Journal of Personality and Social Psychology* 28: 129–137.

Lewis, Catherine, Eric Schaps, and Marilyn Watson. 1995. "Beyond the Pendulum: Creating Caring and Challenging Schools." In *Phi Delta Kappan* 76, no. 7: 547–554.

Lockhart, R., F. I. Craik, and L. Jacoby. 1976. "Depth of Processing, Recall, and Recognition." In *Recall and Recognition*, edited by J. Brown. New York: Wiley.

Macnamara, John. 1972. "Cognitive Basis of Language Learning in Infants." In *Psychological Review* 79: 1–13.

Malinowski, B. 1922. *Argonauts of the Western Pacific*. London: Routledge.

McAleer, Neil. 1989. "On Creativity." In *Omni* 12, no. 2: 22–26.

McLure, Patricia. 1987. "Art and Print in the Classroom." Address delivered at Lesley College Literacy Institute, Cambridge, MA.

Miller, Stephen. 1973. "Ends, Means, and Galumphing: Some Leitmotifs of Play." In *American Anthroplogist* 75, no. 1: 94–103.

Morrison, Toni. 1987. "The Site of Memory." In *Inventing the Truth: The Art and Craft of Memoir*, edited by William Zinsser. Boston: Houghton Mifflin.

Murray, Donald. 1982. *Learning by Teaching: Selected Articles on Writing and Teaching*. Portsmouth, NH: Heinemann-Boynton/Cook.

Nachmanovitch, Stephen. 1990. *Free Play: Improvisation in Life and Art*. Los Angeles: Jeremy P. Tarcher.

Neale, Robert. 1969. *In Praise of Play*. New York: Harper and Row.

Nelson, Katherine. 1993. "Toward a Theory of the Development of Autobiographical Memory." In *Theoretical Advances in the Psychology of Memory*, edited by Andrew Collins et al. Hillsdale, NJ: Erlbaum.

Newkirk, Thomas, and Nancie Atwell. 1988. *Understanding Writing: Ways of Observing, Learning, and Teaching*. 2nd ed. Portsmouth, NH: Heinemann.

Newkirk, Thomas, and Patricia McLure. 1992. *Listening In: Children Talk About Books (And Other Things)*. Portsmouth, NH: Heinemann.

Ohanian, Susan. 1992. "Inside Classroom Structures." In *Vital Signs 3: Restructuring the English Classroom*, edited by James Collins. Portsmouth, NH: Heinemann.

———. 1993. *Garbage Pizza, Patchwork Quilts, and Math Magic*. New York: W. H. Freeman.

Ostrow, Jill. 1994. "Learning to Sit and Listen." In *Teacher Research: The Journal of Classroom Inquiry* 2, no. 1: 107–110.

———. 1995. *A Room with a Different View*. York, ME: Stenhouse.

Panati, Charles. 1987. *Extraordinary Origins of Everyday Things*. New York: Harper and Row.

Papert, Sidney. 1980. *Mindstorms: Children, Computers, and Powerful Ideas*. Brighton: Harvester Press.

Perkins, David. 1981. *The Mind's Best Work*. Cambridge, MA: Harvard University Press.

Polyani, Michael. 1958. *Personal Knowledge*. Chicago: University of Chicago Press.

Power, Brenda Miller. 1992. "Rules Made to Be Broken: Literacy and Play in a Fourth-Grade Setting." In *Journal of Education*. 83–98.

Rief, Linda. 1992. *Seeking Diversity*. Portsmouth, NH: Heinemann.

Rogoff, Barbara. 1993. *Apprenticeship in Thinking: Cognitive Development in Social Context*. New York: Oxford University Press.

Romano, Tom. 1987. *Clearing the Way*. Portsmouth, NH: Heinemann.

Sameroff, Arnold, and Susan McDonough. 1994. "Educational Implications of Developmental Transitions: Revisiting the 5- to 7-Year Shift." In *Phi Delta Kappan* 76, no. 3: 188–193.

Samuels, Mike, and Nancy Samuels. 1975. *Seeing with the Mind's Eye*. New York: Random House.

Schank, Roger, and P. Childers. 1988. *The Creative Attitude: Learning to Ask and Answer the Right Questions*. New York: Macmillan.

Schwartz, Barry, and Daniel Reisberg. 1991. *Learning and Memory*. New York: W. W. Norton.

Short, Kathy, and Carolyn Burke. 1991. *Creating Curriculum: Teachers and Students as a Community of Learners*. Portsmouth, NH: Heinemann.

Soyer, Raphael. 1977. *Diary of an Artist*. Washington, DC: New Republic Books.

Stern, Daniel. 1985. *The Interpersonal World of the Infant*. New York: Basic Books.

———. 1990. *Diary of a Baby*. New York: Basic Books.

Stravinsky, Igor, and Robert Craft. 1962. *Expositions and Developments*. Garden City, NY: Doubleday.

Strickland, Dorothy, and L. M. Morrow. 1989. "Environments Rich in Print Promote Literacy Behavior During Play." In *The Reading Teacher* 43: 178–179.

Ulam, Stan. 1976. *Adventures of a Mathematician*. New York: Scribner.

Vernon, P. E. 1975. *Creativity*. Harmondsworth, UK: Penguin.

Vygotsky, Lev. 1978. *Mind in Society: The Development of Higher Psychological Processes*, edited by M. Cole, V. John-Steiner, and E. Souberman. Cambridge, MA: Harvard University Press.

———. 1986. *Thought and Language*, edited and translated by A. Kozulin. Cambridge, MA: M.I.T. Press.

Wells, Gordon. 1986. *The Meaning Makers: Children Learning Language and Using Language to Learn*. Portsmouth, NH: Heinemann.

Whitmore, Kathryn, and Caryl Crowell. 1994. *Inventing a Classroom: Life in a Bilingual Whole Language Learning Community*. York, ME: Stenhouse.

Winterbourne, Nancy, and Ruth Hubbard. 1990. "Imagination in Literacy: Taking Steps Beyond the Ordinary." Paper presented at Annual Conference for National Council of Teachers of English, Atlanta, GA.

Children's Books

Berger, Barbara. 1984. *Grandfather Twilight*. New York: Philomel Books.

Blume, Judy. 1972. *Otherwise Known as Sheila the Great*. New York: E. P. Dutton.

———. 1974. *The Pain and the Great One*. Scarsdale, NY: Bradbury Press.

Brown, Marc. 1989. *Arthur's Teacher Trouble*. Boston: Little, Brown.

Cleary, Beverly. 1975. *Ramona the Brave*. New York: Scholastic Books.

Dahl, Roald. 1977. *Charlie and the Chocolate Factory*. New York: Bantam/Skylark.

———. 1988. *Matilda*. New York: Puffin Books.

DeAngeli, Marguerite. 1949. *The Door in the Wall*. Garden City, NY: Doubleday.

Eastman, P. D. 1960. *Are You My Mother?* New York: Random House.

Heide, Florence Parry. 1990. *The Day of Ahmed's Secret.* New York: Lothrup, Lee, and Shepard.

Hodges, Margaret. 1984. *Saint George and the Dragon.* Boston: Little, Brown.

Howe, Deborah, and James Howe. 1979. *Bunnicula: A Rabbit-Tale of Mystery.* New York: Atheneum.

Howe, James. 1992. *Return to Howliday Inn.* New York: Atheneum.

Johnson, Crocket. 1955. *Harold and the Purple Crayon.* New York: Harper.

Kimmel, Eric. 1991. *Baba Yaga: A Russian Folktale.* New York: Holiday House.

Lionni, Leo. 1967. *Frederick.* New York: Pantheon.

Lobel, Arnold. 1979. *Days with Frog and Toad.* New York: Scholastic Books.

Minarik, Else. 1957. *Little Bear.* New York: Harper.

Munsch, Robert. 1980. *The Paper Bag Princess.* Willowsdale, Ontario: Firefly Books.

Porter, Connie. 1993. *Addie Learns a Lesson.* Middletown, WI: Pleasant Company Publishing.

Say, Alan. 1988. *A River Dream.* Boston: Houghton Mifflin.

Ward, Lynd. 1973. *The Silver Pony: A Story in Pictures.* Boston: Houghton Mifflin.

White, E. B. 1952. *Charlotte's Web.* New York: Harper and Row.

Index

Other books from Stenhouse you will enjoy...

A ROOM WITH A DIFFERENT VIEW
First Through Third Graders Build Community and Create Curriculum

Jill Ostrow

In *A Room with a Different View*, Jill Ostrow reveals how her class of six- to nine-year-old children physically transformed their classroom, created a community, and completed projects that grew out of the Island and involved everyone in real-world problem solving. Jill presents a new and different approach to curriculum and a philosophy you may want to apply with your own students. Although this classroom will introduce you to some unusual features, it is still one in which traditional school subjects—math, writing, reading, art, and science—are thoroughly integrated in projects that centered on the Island.

1-57110-009-1   Paperback

I SEE WHAT YOU MEAN
Children at Work with Visual Information

Steve Moline

When is an idea best expressed with a picture? And how do you know which kind of picture works best?

In this activity-laden resource book Steve Moline outlines learning strategies that require students to communicate using visual texts. Over one hundred student examples illustrate how students can communicate some concepts better with visual texts than with conventional, word-only texts. These strategies will be especially helpful for students who struggle with writing or who are visual learners.

1-57110-031-8   Paperback

THE BRIDGE TO SCHOOL
Entering a New World

Liz Waterland
Foreword by Glenda L. Bissex

However carefully the first days and weeks of school are planned, a teacher can only imagine what the children will make of it, what feelings and pre-conceptions and fears color their experience. In time, if her teaching succeeds, they will unite and form a community. But so much depends on those first days.

The Bridge to School, an imaginative reconstruction of several months in the life of a school, is an extraordinary view through children's eyes of how it looks and feels to be entering such a daunting, magnetic, enveloping world.

1-57110-020-2   Paperback

For information on all Stenhouse publications,
please write or call for a catalogue.

Stenhouse Publishers
P. O. Box 360
York, Maine 03909
(207) 363-9198